THEY GOT DADDY

THEY GOT DADDY

One Family's Reckoning
with Racism and Faith

—⸻—

SHARON TUBBS

QUARRY BOOKS

An Imprint of
INDIANA UNIVERSITY PRESS

This book is a publication of

Quarry Books

an imprint of
Indiana University Press
Office of Scholarly Publishing
Herman B Wells Library 350
1320 East 10th Street
Bloomington, Indiana 47405 USA

iupress.org

Manufactured in the United States of America

First printing 2023

The author is represented by MacGregor & Luedeke.

Library of Congress Cataloging-in-Publication Data

Names: Tubbs, Sharon, author.
Title: They got daddy : one family's reckoning with racism and faith / Sharon Tubbs.
Description: Bloomington : Quarry Books, an imprint of Indiana
    University Press, 2023. | Includes bibliographical references.
Identifiers: LCCN 2022028144 (print) | LCCN 2022028145 (ebook) | ISBN 9780253064455
    (hardback) | ISBN 9780253064462 (paperback) | ISBN 9780253064479 (ebook)
Subjects: LCSH: United States—Race relations—20th century. | African
    Americans—Social conditions—20th century. | African Americans—Religion—
    History—20th century. | Tubbs, Sharon. | Tubbs, Sharon—Family. | Page
    family. | Reconciliation. | Memory—Social aspects—United States.
Classification: LCC E185.615 .T796 2023 (print) | LCC E185.615
    (ebook) | DDC 305.896/073—dc23/eng/20220728
LC record available at https://lccn.loc.gov/2022028144
LC ebook record available at https://lccn.loc.gov/2022028145

To my mother and father, Granddaddy, Big Mama, Fat Ma,
Grandfather Tubbs, and everyone else who worked to clear the way,
who kept moving and pressing along the rough terrain of our
past to make my path a little smoother.

Tell your children about it in the years to come, and let your
children tell their children. Pass the story down
from generation to generation.
—Joel 1:3 (NLT)

CONTENTS

INTRODUCTION

I DIDN'T REALLY KNOW my grandfather until after he died. I attended his funeral as a little girl and had laid eyes on him at least once a year before then. We never talked much, though, and I can't recall a single conversation between us. Our true introduction came after his passing, through the oral stories and newspaper articles I gathered about him in my adulthood. I wanted to uncover details of a tragedy that featured him, something that rocked my mother's family. My research spoke to my grandfather's challenges as a Black man in the early and mid-1900s, and for some time I thought of the project as strictly historical. I didn't connect his trials during the Jim Crow era with my own twenty-first-century struggles, not initially. Underlying themes of trauma and legacy would link our worlds together much later, as I struggled to process the information and figure out the best way to tell the story.

Decades passed as the facts took shape in my mind and on paper, as different versions of the manuscript. I don't know if the book tarried due to divine providence or procrastination. I like to think of it as providence because, well, it sounds better. Plus, as time progressed, so did technology, increasing my access to information over the years. Yet I had a habit of feverishly working on the project for a while and then setting it aside for a few years, transferring my energy to the more immediate returns of another book idea or a social life. But inevitably some crushing disappointment—a soured relationship or career frustration—forced me to refocus, to concentrate on things that really matter and mean something. I would turn again to my grandfather, always finding substance here, in his untold tale.

The creation process for *They Got Daddy* started narrowly. I would tell the story of Israel Page's five-year legal battle with a white sheriff's deputy named Benjamin Brantley "B. B." Lee, a factual account that remained unspoken. The tale had moved silently through the Page family, feeding into cultural trauma from one generation to the next, until it reached me. Israel Page, of course, was the grandfather I barely knew during his time on earth. Over time, as most stories do, the story swelled and extended beyond the 1950s and into the twenty-first century. *Israel Page v. Brantley Lee* eventually became the catalyst and the framework to explore lingering systemic issues through the experiences of one family, our family. Today, I still wonder about the repercussions resulting from this slice of his life.

Cultural trauma describes the lasting effects of racism on African Americans, or, more generally speaking, it occurs when members of a group endure something horrendous that scars their group consciousness and changes their identity. The concept applies, then, to Jewish people whose ancestors endured the Holocaust, Japanese Americans forced into internment camps, and certainly African Americans in the aftermath of slavery, Jim Crow, and even twenty-first-century tragedies of police brutality. The concept crystallized for me in researching my grandfather's experiences and tying them to the past and the present, including my own behaviors and fears. The record of what happened with B. B. Lee had been hushed, but its ramifications within the family screamed loudly.

Eventually, I realized the story's magnetic draw had as much to do with me as it did with reconstructing a family calamity. Through revelations of my grandfather, I saw more of who I am and *why* I am. Before all of this, I thought of myself in simpler terms, a woman of faith, a creative type, someone who reluctantly gained strength from the challenges that come with being African American and female in America. In different seasons of life, I had socialized, worked, and worshiped with friends white, black, and brown. I treasured diversity and sought it when possible. That was the me I had constructed, and the diagram seemed whole, complete. But history has a way of revealing life's unseen DNA, the stuff at the core of who we are, the marrow that fills our souls without us ever sensing it's there.

Right there, flowing through the family line, racism and the trauma it carries seeped from my grandfather to my mother, uncles and aunts, to me. For the first time, while writing this book, some of my own racial fears and triggers unveiled themselves. Yet, they were not unique. They line up with the unspoken sentiments of many other African Americans. Their commonness, rather than any notion of standing apart, compelled me to include them in what morphed from my grandfather's story to *our* story. And by "our story," I mean my family, yes, but others who can relate also. Historical information I gathered about Black life in the twentieth century dripped with the harsh consequences of oppression. As with my kinfolk, the personal examples of that oppression got lost, some by the intentional erasing of what once was, others by the unintentional neglect to preserve it. That is to say, the examples disappeared from the surface, but they remained with us, on the inside of our being, at the core of our nation's truth and how we perceived it.

I like the way the author and experienced birth doula Jacquelyn Clemmons expresses that cultural trauma can't simply be dismissed or forgotten. "When we consider that we are not only walking around with our own lived experiences and traumas but also those of our ancestors, we must slow down and take a hard, honest look at our past. To truly heal, we must address the cultural trauma that has always been there, shaping our perspective from birth."

Clemmons talked in an interview about how trauma affected her. "I have literally felt my blood boil in certain places, and I don't have any personal reference point for why that would be," she said. "I think there's that epigenetic factor."

In other words, cultural trauma handed down from her ancestors acts as a built-in alarm system, telling her senses that she's in unsafe territory—based not necessarily on reality or her own experience but on that of someone who came before her. "It's the recall," Clemmons said.

At some point, trauma can seep into our DNA and flow through family lineage. And this is true for us all, white, black, and brown people alike. Any traumatic experience can alter behaviors and genetic makeup. But the condition is not irreversible. For cultural trauma, healing may begin on an individual basis, by finding ways to talk about family histories and celebrating good times with loved ones while also acknowledging past struggles. We need to find ways of releasing our pain in a safe space, Clemmons said. "It's the silence that hurts us."

My research became more than ingredients for a book when I considered the impact of cultural trauma and the stigma of black and brown skin in my life. This was a journey of reckoning, of relating and healing that linked my grandfather's experiences with my own. I saw how my fears and emotions mirrored situations my ancestors suffered. Not that I had been blind to these connections before, but I hadn't previously felt them to the same degree. Civil rights legislation swiped away the Whites Only signs, but total equality remained elusive, and the racial events of modern America felt like a proverbial yoke on the neck.

In 2020, the killings of Ahmaud Arbery, Breonna Taylor, and George Floyd occurred in a four-month span. Other fatal shootings followed into 2021, pitting some white police officers against unarmed African Americans. The era marked a shift, an uprising of sorts that yielded protests nationwide, sharp social media debates of free speech and so-called cancel culture. America revealed its heart as divided, its future headed backward toward a stark segregation of ideals. All the while, some Americans tried to simply ignore racism for the sake of denial, white privilege, and supremacy. The combination of events was not merely injustice, not for me, not for other African Americans whose families carried stories like my grandfather's. For many of us, these tragedies equaled triggers, awakening the trauma inside of us, sparking emotional pleas for help and hope, eliciting passions that our white friends and allies could not fathom because their bloodline lacked the tainted plasma of discrimination.

The book, then, served to chart my racial foundations, finding that my story not only linked to my grandfather's by DNA but that our actual experiences were intertwined. For that reason, the book switches from one chapter to the next, exploring my grandfather's narrative and family dynamic, followed by that of my generation. Each chapter uses terms common during its given era for the purpose of authenticity. For scenes set in the 1950s and previously, I refer to Black people as "Negroes," and there are scant references to being "colored." For modern experiences, I use the terms "African American" and "Black," in keeping with the era.

Aside from cultural trauma, my grandfather's battle also creates an opportunity to further explore the effects of racism on the Black body. After a car accident, my grandfather lay on a hospital cot with a crushed arm for hours waiting for treatment. White doctors and nurses treated other incoming white patients first. The essence of that scene plays out in modern times with some medical professionals, although less blatantly so. These days, studies reveal implicit bias in our medical profession, where Black patients are undermedicated for pain when compared to white patients. Some professionals subconsciously absorbed myths that African Americans have thicker skin, don't feel pain as deeply, or that we would abuse prescribed drugs more than other groups.

Just as my grandfather's experience in the 1950s can be linked to systemic racism, other examples link past to present. The eugenics movement took hold when racist white doctors and legislators nationwide decided to sterilize poor people, criminals, and the mentally ill—but mostly Black women. The women would show up for surgeries, expecting doctors to correct some other problem, only to find out later that they'd performed hysterectomies. It seems almost too far-fetched or removed in time to believe these days. Yet a similar conspiracy reportedly occurred not long ago. In 2020, a whistleblower exposed a doctor who performed hysterectomies on undocumented women detained by US

Immigration and Customs Enforcement (ICE). Some inmates needed medical attention, and authorities transported them to a certain doctor. According to the whistleblower, that doctor performed hysterectomies without permission.

In 2017, I had surgery and mentioned the procedure to a friend of mine, a lawyer and one of the smartest women I know. She then told a story of how surgery became taboo in her family when doctors stole the wombs of two Black female relatives during the eugenics era decades earlier. She didn't know the details, but the story survived generations, creating cultural trauma that automatically shunned invasive medical procedures. It came as no surprise to me, then, when African Americans initially ranked among the most resistant groups to taking COVID-19 vaccines. Of course, we were. Records of the eugenics movement and the Tuskegee Experiment baked into the culture a deep mistrust for American medicine.

The Tuskegee Experiment began in 1932 and involved Black men who had contracted syphilis. Researchers wanted to study the disease's effects on their bodies. Yet, when professionals eventually found a cure for the disease, researchers refused to tell the men about it, allowing many to die instead for the sake of a medical study. This happened in Macon County, Alabama, just 120 miles from where my grandparents lived. In the twenty-first century, some African Americans didn't even know the particulars of Tuskegee or eugenics, yet they'd heard enough. Mainstream schools and other educational institutions hadn't taught the stories, which only heightened their mystery and lent credence to the concept of an evil system. Some Black people cited these scandals as the reasons to avoid vaccination. Indeed, generations later these events live on culturally, as proof of necessary skepticism in the US government and the vaccines its leaders pushed to solve a pandemic.

Another past-present link, my maternal great grandmother, Harriet Walker, died giving birth to twins. Midwives in those days had a hard time maneuvering complications with single births, let alone when two babies crowded the womb. Medical procedures for childbirth have advanced. Yet Black women and their babies still experience comparatively high rates of maternal and infant mortality. In spring 2020, I became a leader for a social service agency that educates underserved people in nutrition and mental health, as well as combatting chronic conditions. My nonprofit work led me to observe trends in health inequities, including high rates of death for Black pregnant women and their babies. By 2019, for instance, Black women in Indiana died giving birth at the same rate as women in some underdeveloped nations. Despite the lapse of time, maternal and infant mortality remained a major issue since my great grandparents lived and died a century ago.

These national past-present links sharpened my purview to see likeness in my own personal experiences, which I explore in the pages to come. Now I could see how unspoken events that involved race and class in my youth left their mark on my womanhood. I understood how my grandparents' and parents' lives fed into the broader picture of me. There was no car accident or lawsuit, as was the case with my grandfather, but for me it was the trip to the zoo in elementary school, the women "shouting" at church, accusations while shopping for an outfit, the assignment to cover a Klan rally as a young journalist. None of these situations compelled me to deep conversations or intellectual debates at the time. I wanted to forget a few of them, to push them away, yet they stayed with me. Over the years, I remembered them clearly. And now I know why. These episodes became part of me. In the same way, my mother and uncles and aunts didn't speak of that legal case. They didn't rush to recall it or bring it to mind. But each of them had a certain relationship with it. For some it settled in and quietly, unknowingly, made its way into their decisions and outlooks on life in America.

Still, so much more filled my research than oppression and fear. Equally engrained in our story are the closer times, the family reunions and bonds formed through laughter and perseverance. The oral family stories that I had heard for years without appreciating them with their laughter and cultural swagger. These were the memories that relatives retold at family reunions, during dinner after a funeral service, while sitting on the front porch to catch a spring breeze. In any retelling of my grandfather's story, I knew I had to include some of these historical snapshots to convey the strength of the Black family, the overcoming spirit that refuses to let the pangs of the world steal their joy, their zeal for living. Black families relish stories about this uncle or that cousin, about the sass of this old man, the strength of grandmothers called Madear (short for "Mother Dear") or Nana or Big Mama. The Black family and its members have always amounted to more than the heaviness of our racial battles.

Often, these stories of strength and fond memories rest within a reverence for God. My grandparents planted the seeds for strong spiritual convictions passed down to my mother and to me. The same is true for millions of Black Americans for whom faith is the balm in Gilead that relieves suffering. None of us has seen God face-to-face, yet we tend to lean on him, believe in him more deeply than the faces of those who rejected, belittled, or berated us. With faith, we survived the harshest of conditions from seventeenth-century fields, to the protest marches of the sixties, to the shootings that preceded the Black Lives Matter movement. African Americans are more likely to read the Bible and commit to faith than any other group, according to the Pew Research Center.

We cherish the notion that something bigger than us and our problems brings meaning to life in America, even when circumstances belittle our existence. I couldn't tell *They Got Daddy* without including the role of faith and how my grandparents wielded it back in the day, how my mother established religion as a staple for living in our home.

Faith buttressed the Page family's migration from the South to the Midwest—just as it had for millions of other African Americans who landed in Cincinnati, Detroit, Chicago, or Pittsburgh, where Blacks flocked throughout the 1900s for social and economic relief from Jim Crow. They hoped for more, fleeing the effects of oppression in the South—effects that we still don't fully understand, despite all our studies, intellectual reports, and analyses. In the end, our family's destination changed for generations to come, partly because of what happened to my grandfather in an era just before the civil rights movement congealed.

Today, belief in God continues to provide a tool for emotional stability for our next generation in a society that can be cruel and unjust. God's premise of human equality prevails, even as history repeats itself with white supremacists again gaining credibility in America, the value of Black lives seems to be minimized, and immigrants of color are shunned by a nation itself founded by immigrants. Israel Page's experience allows me—*us*—to understand how the loved ones of nine Black people murdered in 2015 at a church in Charleston, South Carolina, immediately forgave the proud, racist shooter. Of course, they forgave him. They *needed* to forgive. We all do, more so for ourselves than anyone else. When pushing through my own challenges, the faith and perseverance of my ancestors compels me more than ever to deepen my own belief system, seeing forgiveness, steadfastness, and the will to take on the Goliaths of our time as the path to turn our narrative from despair to hope. No, ours is not a story that fits neatly into social media memes or surface, quick-fix inspiration. It's a story of endurance, of overcoming life's deepest pains and seeming failures. It's a true reality show that we all participate in at some point, no matter our skin color or social class.

Throughout this project, I felt the complexity of emotions, including the pain that my relatives must have worked through and that people of color live with regardless of our generation or time. The defeat of discrimination. The frustration and belittling of injustice. But also, I felt the reasons why African Americans possess pride and distinction in who we are, nonetheless. The passion for our culture. The hope and confidence found through faith.

In the end, my grandfather was not the Martin Luther King Jr. I wrote about in a middle-school essay. He was no Medgar Evers or Thurgood Marshall. He was just a Black man who wanted to take care of his family and live his life in a small country town, a man who believed strongly in a God much bigger than us all. He was this guy living at a time when an unjust system threatened to use his skin color to steal his greatness and hope, in much the same way that injustice threatens us all. That same threat never stopped breathing through my grandfather's children. It still breathes in me today. Now, through these pages, I exhale.

THEY GOT DADDY

—⚉—

CHAPTER ONE

GONE, JUST GONE

HE DIDN'T COZY UP to them right away that day, not likely—not for two strangers who weren't from around these parts. He kept his distance, there on the porch, content to peer at them, offer his typical greeting for white men: "Boss?"

They were looking for a man called Israel, they told him, Israel Page.

Could this have something to do with the court case? The possibility had to enter his mind. It was January 15, 1959, four and a half years since the accident and the injury, since he could drill a well and bring home a decent paycheck. In some ways he had recovered. He'd gotten his mind back, his thinking straight, and he could still preach, that's for sure. But he'd lost a lot, too. His arm hung limp at his side, useless as a loaf of hog headcheese. Still, there was a measure of courage to him. That's what it took, courage, for a Negro to go up against a white sheriff's deputy in Alabama over the whole thing. Now, in less than twenty-four hours, Israel Page would get the trial he'd waited for, and he expected justice to side with him.

With all that in mind, compounded by the racial tensions of the day, it's a wonder that he let down his guard at all, that he opened up to those white strangers the way he did. But, indeed, he did. Faith assured him that the Lord lingered near. He trusted God to protect him with the kind of trust that drives all the fear out of a man and, some might say, a little of his common sense, too.

Whatever the reason, he told the men that if they were looking for Israel Page, they'd found him. You could imagine their relief, since they'd searched all over Browns and Uniontown by then, driving through backcountry roads. They didn't live in this town, they said, and they heard he preached to the Negroes.

That's how the conversation started anyway. He told the men about churches nearby, talking easily and for a good while, as he was known to do, and somehow the conversation turned to hunting dogs. He knew everything there was to know about hunting dogs. He had a few good beagles of his own, and he'd let them loose and follow them into the woods to sniff out the scent of easy prey—rabbit, coon, or even squirrel—which his wife, Margaret, turned into dinner. That's when the men told him about a beagle they had. Matter of fact, they said, it was in their car, parked over there by the road. Would he come out, take a look?

Now, Margaret might have witnessed all this if she hadn't been prepping for the next day. She busied herself inside the house, styling her hair with the hot pressing comb, parting it and straightening each section in preparation for their courthouse appearance. The pungent smell of smoked hair filled the wood board house. Unlike her husband, she would've wanted to get far away from their visitors. She didn't make small talk with white folks. They'd grin to your face in the daylight, then cackle through slits in white sheets come night. She kept on parting and pressing her hair, pressing and parting.

It couldn't have been too long before she noticed something wrong, though. The voices outside had stopped. She walked to the front door but saw nobody there, no one outside in view at all. She stepped onto the porch, then down the steps and into the yard, neck turning, voice calling out the nickname most called her husband: "Preacher?"

She walked fast around the yard, scanned the edge of the property, peering across fields, hoping for a glimpse of him. She looked down the road until it curved and disappeared. No Preacher. Before long, their latest family car kicked up dirt coming toward the house. Inside, Robert Lee and Willie James, two of the older boys, along with a family friend, were returning from a trip uptown to see what they called a "picture show" back then.

Now they saw the worried look on their mother's face.

Had they seen Preacher walking up the road?

They told her no. Willie James scoped the surroundings, his sense for detail absorbing the scene, as his younger brother Robert Lee stood alongside, slender and tall. No, Daddy wasn't on the road, they said. Hadn't seen anybody driving since they turned off Highway 80 onto the dirt pathway leading home.

No Preacher?

No, ma'am.

None of it made sense. Margaret's mind whirled, piecing everything together. On the day before the big trial, men come to the house, asking for

Preacher—white men. Then all of a sudden he's gone, not a stitch of him anywhere, and as laid-back as he was, Preacher never walked that fast to get anywhere.

She and the boys inched to the edge of the red dirt, looked down the path time and again, satisfying themselves that they hadn't missed something. Could he have turned down one of the side cuts, heading to the house of a friend or relative? Soon, they would enlist neighbors in a search throughout the area.

The younger kids still bided time inside the house, but eventually they, too, would catch on that something wasn't right, and everything was wrong. Margaret, a tall thick woman with a strong back for picking crops, killing chickens, and milking cows—and perhaps an even stronger heart—opened her mouth and called out again and again: "Preacher? Pree-cherrr!"

—✺—

CHAPTER TWO

HISTORY BREATHES AGAIN

The courthouse clerk in Selma, Alabama, stared at me blankly. Not that I blamed her. A Black woman with the diction of a northerner had just marched down the long hallway, talking about a grandfather whose name was the Jewish holy land.

"Yes, Israel Page," I repeated, "spelled like the country, Israel."

I cleared my throat and kept talking, despite the silence. After all, I'd driven nine hours from Florida to ask a simple question—a question that seemed a long shot to family members and that I knew would sound ridiculous to the woman standing across the counter. Nevertheless, a question I had to pose.

"Is there any way to find a lawsuit filed by a man named Israel Page?" I said, building confidence for the next part. "A case filed, um, sometime between 1954 and 1959?"

"Nineteen fifty-ni-un?" Her voice mimicked Dolly Parton or some other white southern-belle type, only softer.

I clarified the name, partly to fill an awkward silence. Then she sighed heavily and shook her head. Anything that old would be boxed up in the basement, she told me. Some records had been lost, the rest unorganized, a mess down there. She looked around, as if assessing the busyness of the scene. No one stood in line behind me. She'd give it a try, she said. She'd sure try. She pushed a notepad across the counter for me to write down the name and the dates, then she disappeared down the hall.

I waited in the sterile room, as other clerks beyond the counter talked on phones or wrote on pads or sifted through file cabinets. Decades had passed since I got the first hint that something illegal, something tragic, had happened to my grandfather. Back then, I was a little girl in the latter stages of elementary school, living in my childhood home in Fort Wayne, Indiana. My mother and I sat on the couch, watching the news on our wooden floor model TV, when a cloud of silly dunce caps paraded across the screen. The Ku Klux Klan had a permit to march somewhere in the state. This was the 1980s. I thought of nice white teachers, guidance counselors, and classmates at school, so the news story confused me. White people still hated Black people? The KKK, those scary men with the white sheets from the Black history films—those people still existed?

For sure, Mama said. And that's when it slipped out of her, almost like a distant memory: "They got Daddy."

She tried to end the discussion then with a nod and tight lips, as if nothing more need be explained. But I pressed.

"What do you mean they got him?"

"The Klan—they came to the house, and they tricked him, and they got him," she said.

"But why?"

"Had something to do with the sheriff," she said, "but I wasn't there." She explained that she was staying for a while in Faunsdale, a small Alabama town about five miles away. She had gone to help her great-aunt around the house and was there when it all happened.

She didn't say much more after that, partially because she couldn't recall it all. She hadn't spoken about it in so long. Yet the feelings left behind remained raw. Gradually, over the years, my questions squeezed out a little more detail, then just a little more. I asked uncles and aunts what they remembered. Some didn't want to dredge up bad feelings. Others revealed only scant information still in memory. The family, I realized, had separated this thing about white men "getting Daddy" from their tales of life back in the day. The details remained as vague as the memory of a thing that happens a lifetime before. The pain and anger some still felt remained. It spoke to me clearly, precisely. I heard it in their tone, saw it in the slits their eyes made when questions took them back to the scene. Whatever happened when those people got Preacher Page made a mark on his children and, by extension, his grandchildren, too—even me, even before I realized the impact.

I grew up in a midsize midwestern city, in a neighborhood about fifteen minutes' walking distance from downtown. White people fled the area once African Americans started unloading boxes and setting up bedposts there. Most of our neighbors, like us, belonged to the Great Migration. We'd all arrived in Indiana riding a wave with more than six million Blacks who relocated from the South, moving to the North, the Midwest, and the West between 1915 and 1970. Our neighboring families hailed from Mississippi, Georgia, Arkansas, and Alabama.

For many families, summertime meant a car trip down south at some point. Our clan, the Tubbses, always stopped at my maternal grandparents' house first. I knew we were close when the McDonald's arches vanished, the highways narrowed to hilly paths, the Piggly Wiggly grocery store emerged, and the scent of cow dung seeped through open windows. Once there, I avoided the nameless hunting dogs in the yard and stepped carefully to avoid any semblance of dog or cow waste matting the grass—the unnecessary actions of a "city gal," as my grandmother called my sister and me. Big Mama, the name us grandkids called her, typically sat on the porch, churning butter or snapping beans or just rocking in her chair, talking and laughing with people distantly connected on our complex family tree.

Soon, I would see my grandfather, although there would be no meaningful interaction between us. Most times I moved out of his way, never sitting on his lap or talking to him much, not that I recall. Instead, fat mosquitoes and sweltering heat frame memories of our sojourn down south, not to mention the pitch-black nights of rural Alabama—and Big Mama. Her presence commanded our best, most respectful behavior: *Yes, ma'am; no, ma'am.* But my grandfather? He had just one good arm; the other hung loosely inside its shirt-sleeve, and for some reason this frightened my immature mind. I stole glances of him from the corner of my eye.

On more than one occasion, an uncle or aunt looked around the house and noticed him missing from the scene. "Where's Daddy?" they'd say, walking fast around the front room with troubled expressions. Then the commotion, the men scurrying about, searching out back and across the yard from where the chickens pecked. They trotted along the dirt road and peered across the fields. My mother and aunts paced the worn floor tile with worry on their faces and hands on their hips. Sooner or later either someone found him or he reappeared of his own accord looking dazed and unaware. After those men had gotten him, the family had feared these days would come.

The grandfather I knew sat quietly in his pine high-back chair with its seat of woven straw. At ages five and six, I'd ease from his presence then, move to the porch or the kitchen or some other room in Big Mama's house. To me, he was the man with one arm who got lost, who couldn't find his way. My mother told me how he used to preach and dig wells, how he'd called her his "thousand-dollar

In the 1960s, the Page family built this house in Uniontown, after moving from Browns. Siblings who migrated to the Midwest and North brought their children here for annual visits. *Page family photo*

girl" in childhood. I doubted he even knew me as Julia's youngest, though, and the distant look in his eye unnerved my young view of normalcy.

Then, in July 1980, our vacation down south turned into a funeral trip. People drove from New York, Michigan, and Indiana until they reached a dot on the map called Uniontown, Alabama, about thirty miles from Selma. The family church couldn't hold them all, so the ceremony took place in a larger sanctuary where old-timers crowded the wood pews. My grandfather, the patriarch of a farming family with thirteen sons and daughters, had died. He was seventy-two. I was seven. The choir sang, and the soles of kiddie patent leather shoes clicked against the wood plank floors. Up front, an open casket displayed the body of the Rev. Israel Page, eyes closed and finally at rest.

I did not know then that he'd liked to read books when he was younger, just like I did. I had no concept of him working for a well-drilling company in town or how his boss considered him an expert in the field. I couldn't relate to his love of rural living, an affinity for the country that left no taste for visiting the North to see its urban enclaves with their cookie-cutter houses, sidewalks, and fast-food restaurants. In my young mind, the racial stuff, the slavery and the prejudice, happened down south long ago, or at least that's what our school-books said. Reality clicked the day I saw the TV news story about that Klan rally. My parents had warned of prejudice and its deceitful ways of chasing us, of trying to steal our dignity and our faith.

For my mother, much of that perspective originated with her father, a man who had long made peace with the grave when history and research introduced the two of us. From the day I heard something mysterious had happened to him, the urge for us to meet never left me. The refrain "*They got Daddy, they got Daddy*" played in my head, and my heart, too. I remembered it when I wrote about Martin Luther King Jr. for my middle-school essay contest. I thought about it while watching civil rights documentaries on TV. I wondered about the "story" of it while studying journalism in college and occasionally through-out my career from newspaper reporter to editor. Whatever happened robbed me and my cousins of getting to know him better, as a grandfather, as a man. I needed to piece his story together and reclaim a slice of the relationship that might have been.

In 2005, the time felt right for my first trip to Selma. Coincidentally, the an-nual Page family reunion would be held nearby, in Uniontown. I hadn't attended a family reunion since college. The social gathering later that weekend with relatives, the fish fry, the soul food banquet and dedication ceremony, the DJ and the latest line dance—it all dwindled to afterthought as I drove from a Best Western off Highway 80 to the Dallas County Courthouse in downtown Selma.

My parents warned me not to get my hopes up. In the years leading up to the trip, I'd broached the subject with family members to get as many details as pos-sible. The strangest part: I had to call my grandfather by a title that never existed between us while he lived. As a child, I found no reason to call on him or give him a spoken title. Now an adult, I decided to call him Granddaddy, a name that made him feel closer in death than he'd ever been in life. "I just wanted to ask a couple questions about Granddaddy," I'd tell uncles and aunts. I questioned them as if conducting interviews for an article, using best journalism practices to gather information. Keep the tone thoughtful. Have a conversation. Encour-age the sources to tell memories, in hopes they would reveal gems beyond the scope of my questions.

I learned of his easygoing personality, that he didn't have much of a penchant for field work, and that he pastored backwoods churches on rotating Sundays.

The author, Sharon Tubbs, poses in front of the Edmund Pettus Bridge during a research trip to Selma, Alabama, in 2009. *Sharon Tubbs photo*

Deep in the facts of it all, an uncle just happened to mention the most key of details one day. Granddaddy had hired a lawyer, Uncle Willie James revealed. And this lawyer filed a civil lawsuit. We narrowed the dates, and I kept a five-year window to be sure. It was the best news I'd heard—the possibility of a paper trail with concrete information to bolster the verbal histories I collected.

Now, as I waited for the courthouse clerk to return, I didn't know what to do with my hands, or my thoughts for that matter. She took a while, at least fifteen or twenty minutes, which felt like an hour. To calm my nerves, I closed my eyes and said a discreet prayer. I believed in divine destiny, and I wondered if the time I'd spent poring over public records and background checks in my career had led me here, to a stately building in downtown Selma, just blocks from the Edmund Pettus Bridge. Law enforcement officers had attacked six hundred civil rights demonstrators on that bridge decades earlier, including a young John Lewis, who later became the longtime US congressman from Georgia. They swung billy clubs and sprayed tear gas on a day that became known as "Bloody Sunday." (I would later go to that bridge and ask other tourists to shoot my photo standing beneath its sign. My father appreciated the bridge's historic value more than I did at the time. He took the photo to a Walgreens, had it blown up and framed. One critique, he offered, considering the occasion: "It's a good picture," he told me, "but you shouldn't have smiled.")

I wondered if my journalism training had been as much for this very moment as it had been for the sake of writing about that corrupt car mechanic, the latest noise ordinance, or the sneaky political tactics of a small-town mayor. Had my work ushered me here, to a story with a greater personal purpose than the public's right to know? This story would allow me to process the present through the past, to frame modern examples of racism in the context of what my ancestors experienced and passed down to us. This story would reveal parts of who I am, as a Black woman in America, by discovering who my grandfather was.

Footsteps click-clacked against the floor, and the clerk reappeared, handing me a long blue file folder. "*You*," she said, "are one lucky lady."

The folder felt thin but sturdy, almost new, between my fingers, the papers inside white and crisp enough for a paper cut, like they had stiffened after being filed away and untouched for all those years. My heart pounded. I skimmed the documents at first, just to take in a little bit, before reproducing the folder's contents on a copy machine and driving back to the hotel room, nervously, carefully, as if transporting the most valuable jewel. I kicked my feet up on the bed and read this time, every line, gathering dates and other details to follow up for more information. The next day, I drove to the Selma library. Knowing how newspapers worked, I chose a few dates to search first, then perused years of articles on microfilm. The stories told of Eisenhower, Russia, and communism, of cotton mills and dairy maidens, of segregation, the mysterious "accidental" deaths of Black men—and of a "Browns Negro" named Israel "Preacher" Page. My mother's words had, indeed, been true. Yes, there were white men, likely with Klan or other white supremacist ties. And on a brisk winter day in 1959, they got him. But Granddaddy's struggle actually began during the sweltering summer of 1954 in a most unremarkable way.

CHAPTER THREE

—⟋ɷ⟍—

DRILLING DEEP

BIG MAMA USUALLY woke up first, with the groans that transition a woman from a night's sleep to a new dawn. Eventually, she would make her way to the kitchen and pour kerosene in the lamp to give off some light while she tossed wood in the stove to start a fire for cooking. She'd mix the flour and baking powder and water, then knead her dough.

By the time Granddaddy walked in, fresh golden biscuits would be puffing side by side in a tin pan.

"Mooorning," he'd say in his trademark pinched drawl.

Big Mama would respond likewise, then put a couple biscuits on his plate, positioning cane syrup in his reach for sopping. He loved eggs, too, but strangely preferred them sunny-side up, not scrambled or boiled, as was more typical of Negroes at the time. When they had eggs, Big Mama put those runny yolks on his plate, or, knowing him, he just grabbed one raw, cracked open the shell, and swallowed it. "Good for you," he'd say when the kids winced.

After breakfast, Granddaddy would lumber around the house a bit, listening and watching as the kids stirred the place to life again. It was a simple life by today's standards but one that made them grateful. Israel Page married Margaret Warren in 1927. Both grew up in the same area, working fields just a few miles apart. By the 1950s, their proverbial quiver full of children at home had dwindled. The older siblings had grown up and moved away, leaving just seven of them plus a granddaughter living in the house.

Granddaddy's usual routine between eating his biscuits and getting out of the house included sitting and listening to an old family radio. Stilted voices announced homegoing services at area funeral homes and the weather forecast. This day, July 15, 1954, would be a hot one, ranging from the nineties up to a

Israel and Margaret Page. (Photo was taken sometime before July 1954.)
Page family photo

hundred degrees in parts of the state. But summer heat never stopped country
folks from working hard—they couldn't afford not to—and sometime that day
Granddaddy set out to earn a living.

He'd worked for Cecil Radford and his father for nearly thirty years, since
before the Lord called him to the pulpit. The Radford family owned a well

An aging sign off Highway 80 advertises Radford & Son Water Wells, the family-owned company that employed Israel Page for nearly thirty years. *Sharon Tubbs photo*

company that went by various names across generations, such as Cecil Radford & Son Water Well Contractors or Radford & Son Water Wells. It operated in offices near the Highway 80 corridor in Selma, and on this day, Radford had a job to be done with Preacher Page's name on it. Over the years, Granddaddy positioned himself as an asset to the company. He knew how to work the drill, digging deep into the earth's layers on a quest for the good groundwater beneath.

I first spoke with Cecil's son, Robert Radford, during a research trip in December 2009. I drove up and down Highway 80, between Uniontown and Selma, taking in the scenery fifty years after *they got him*. I hadn't expected to see the old blue and white sign, but there it was: "Radford & Son Water Wells." I parked, stood on the dirt landscape, and took pictures, feeling closer than ever to Granddaddy's world outside of the old homestead. Newspaper ads noted different business addresses for the Radfords over the passage of time. And there, in front of this sign, I imagined my grandfather driving his old Chevy to whichever meeting place beckoned, reporting for work.

Of course, by the time of my visit, Cecil Radford had already "gone on to glory," as my elders would say. But white people who grew up in Alabama in the early twentieth century, especially those who lived well, seemed less inclined to relocate elsewhere like us migrant Blacks. Later, in my hotel room, I flipped through a phone book—yes, they still had those in Alabama back then. I dialed several numbers before connecting with a "Radford, Robert" and telling the person on the other end my name. I was looking for Cecil Radford's relatives, I told him, the Radfords who owned the well-drilling company off 80.

The man identified himself as Cecil's son, and I started the spiel. "Mr. Radford, I'm researching a legal case involving my grandfather, Israel Page," I said. "For more than thirty years, he worked for your father, Mr. Cecil Radford—"

"I remember your grandfather," he said.

"You do?" My voice rose an entire octave. I couldn't help the mixture of excitement and shock. Of course, I had hoped he would remember but figured it unlikely. The reporter in me hit the jackpot, a source outside of the family who could speak about the subject objectively and contemporaneously.

"I do," he confirmed. "I knew Israel Page."

We talked only briefly that day, though, because he didn't feel well, too pained to focus on remembering and storytelling. I wrote him a letter after returning to Tampa, my home at the time. I waited and waited but heard nothing and figured I never would. Then, two years later, Robert Radford called the cell number I'd put in that letter. He'd tucked it away, then forgotten about it until recently rifling through old paperwork. He knew he had to call me back. Granddaddy, he said, "meant a lot to my father, so if he meant a lot to my father, he meant a lot to me."

Granddaddy worked for the Radfords from the time he was a teenager, yet I never imagined a relationship closer than simply employer-to-employee. Besides skin color, a stark economic line separated the Pages and the Radfords. My grandparents survived with a houseful of kids on sharecropping and well-drilling checks. The Radfords, on the other hand, lived among the elite in nearby Selma. Almost reading my mind, Robert Radford hurriedly added that the Radfords hadn't always known prosperity. He spoke about the Great Depression of the 1930s, when poverty had touched his family just as it had the rest of the country.

"We were all on hard times, as was your grandfather," he said. "It was hand-to-mouth, taking a job wherever you could get a job."

Radford said one of his aunts made soup every day, and he toted a can with a lid on it, ready to fill it up for the day's meal. In those times, people couldn't pay to have wells drilled, so the Radfords moved often when the rent was due.

Even then, Cecil Radford and his well-drilling father before him, Oscar "O. B." Radford, built their lives on the foundation of their Christian faith. They gave what they could in the church offering bucket, Robert Radford said. In the early lean years, that meant giving just a pittance, or "the widow's mite," he said, borrowing a phrase from the Bible.

Around the same time, the federal government developed a housing project called Gee's Bend Farms for struggling Negroes on a former plantation. The government needed a company to drill wells for the new development, and only two companies bid on it, the Radfords being one of them. Cecil Radford had two men working for him at the time, but he knew he needed to work faster, Robert Radford said.

"He went and got Israel and brought him into Selma," Radford said. "They built another drilling rig, a water-well drilling rig, and they put wheels on it." Cecil then hired two more men and assigned them to follow and listen to Granddaddy. "He was a smart man," Radford said. "We all admired and respected him. He was one of us, so to speak."

As the Depression lifted, the well-drilling company gained clientele and employees. At one point, the Radfords had seven Black workers, Radford told me. Many times through the years, Granddaddy dined with the Radfords, right along with Robert, his brother, sister, mother, and father. (Incidentally, the "son" in Radford & Son was Robert's older brother, John Radford Sr.)

"Whenever we had food, he sat down and ate with us," Radford said. "On Monday morning, before they would leave to go to work, my mother served everybody a big breakfast." As a matter of fact, Granddaddy brought at least one Radford breakfast custom home to Browns. He'd tasted sunny-side up eggs at the Radford house, according to his granddaughter who grew up in the Page home. He decided he liked his eggs better that way.

"If you worked for us and you were in our home, you sat at the table with us," Radford said, adding that his family never leaned toward white supremacy.

Granddaddy stashed hard candies, so he could hand them to little boy Radford and other kids along the way. Radford chuckled, thinking about it now. "He just kept those in his pockets, and when he'd see us, he'd give us one, and we'd just hang onto him like he was Jesus."

For a time, neither the Pages nor the Radfords had a phone, so on a few occasions, when Cecil Radford needed help, a second opinion, or just to get a message through, he went to Granddaddy. "I remember my father and I going to his place, to his house, down around about Uniontown, Alabama, talking to him on two or three occasions," Radford said. "They had old-fashioned wire gates around there."

Before Granddaddy had a car of his own, Cecil Radford sometimes showed up at the Pages' door alone to pick him up for a well-drilling job, my mother told me. Then they'd get to work. Granddaddy and Cecil drilled pure water wells, drained from below the "Selma chalk," Robert Radford said. It could take nearly a week to drill a well. Sometimes, they'd hit a rock down there. They'd have to "bump, bump, bump" to get through the granite shelf, he said. Granddaddy and Cecil knew where that shelf was. When they had a tough well like that, they'd charge more. They had to use this rotary machine and rework the drill bit.

"Your grandfather would lean over that well, and he'd feel with his hand. He had nice, big tender hands."

He'd been in the business so long that Granddaddy could rub the grains of earth between his fingertips and determine by the coarseness or softness if they'd drilled far enough. "They were professional," Radford said.

Countless cultural norms and economic factors stood in the way of his father and my grandfather having a traditional friendship. They did not meet up for a cup of coffee. Their families didn't go on couples' vacations or do many of the things we'd think of today that friends would. But after working with Grand-daddy through years lean and prosperous, one thing Radford said he knew about his father, Cecil Radford: "He loved your grandfather."

I can't presume the feelings in my grandfather's heart, but, if nothing more, a deep loyalty had to exist for the Radfords. They escorted him through his young adult years into middle age. So, when it came to that day in 1954, Granddaddy ate his breakfast, listened to the radio, snapped his trademark suspenders, and readied to do what he'd done for decades—get to work for the Radfords. He'd bought a car of his own now, a used black Chevy from W. T. Buck. The family used to live on Buck's farm, sharecropping cotton. That meant they picked the cotton and gave it to him. The crop could yield several hundred dollars per bail back then, at least that's how Uncle Willie James remembers it. That money, of course, went to Buck. Willie James worked close beside Granddaddy to manage the farming. Buck, he said, profited from the cotton, while the family received just a small portion. For a time, Buck deducted from the family's take to pay off that Chevy until Granddaddy owned it. They'd moved from Buck's place to live on a plot of land that Coleman Long owned in Browns between Uniontown, the closest city to the west, and Selma, farther to the east.

I can see Granddaddy cranking that Chevy's engine, then steering along, watching his native land glide across the windshield like landscapes in a country museum. The caramel-colored and speckled cows munching on blades of green grass, mooing lazily across fields that stretched for acres. The steeple-topped church houses at the ends of footpaths that wound through tall trees and brush. The wooden bridges that creaked a little at the weight of his car passing over a lake or stream. The familiar smell of oak and dung filling his nostrils, the hot breeze streaming through the car window.

He headed for Highway 80, eastbound toward the well-drilling office. He may have intended to talk to Cecil Radford for a bit. Or did his schedule include other plans that day? A member of the local Prince Hall Lodge, at some point he might have joined with other "brothers" of the fraternal order, a branch of Freemasonry for Negroes. Granddaddy also liked to drop by the Sundown Ranch, a Negro-owned store with snacks by day, where men gathered to talk about a little of this and a little of that. (By nighttime and on weekends, the Sundown turned into a watering hole and party spot, so Preacher Page steered clear after dusk.)

People all over town knew Granddaddy as a talker, the kind of man with comments tucked away for startup conversations with Blacks and whites, too. The kind who passed out candies to kids, no matter their skin color. Yet Grand-daddy's tendency to mingle with whites didn't carry over to his wife or children. For the most part, the Pages woke up with the dawn, went to the kitchen, and picked out their breakfast biscuits, at least until the last one was gone. Later they went outdoors to work the fields or chase each other down dirt patches or climb trees. The girls made up the beds, stretching the sheets tight and tucking the corners neat enough to impress a military sergeant, because that's how Big Mama wanted it. They cooked, too, washed, and ironed. During the harvest season, they picked cotton or peanuts or whatever grew in the fields. In the off season, they caught the school bus with Big Mama's brother, Uncle Scoe, behind the wheel. Some in the family believe "Scoe" was a shortened southern pronunciation of Score, but no one really knows. Its spelling and origin faded long ago, right along with other nicknames from that era, such as Huh-naw, Skeechi, Geech, and Toot. Away from school, Big Mama's boys, like their father, met up with whites for farming jobs or hard labor to earn their paychecks. But they didn't carry candies in their pockets for the boss's kids.

Granddaddy came from a people who still remembered what slavery looked like, what it felt like. They knew the body aches from working long hours in the field. Their minds knew the spirit-breaking toll of being looked upon as animals and property. When people come from a way of life as evil as that, I imagine some just feel grateful it's over, that they escaped or that God didn't blow breath into their bodies before the Civil War. They wouldn't focus on the injustice that lingers, not necessarily. That was Granddaddy. Grateful for what he had, for what he could do, without pondering all the privileges racism prevented. Others wanted more. They wanted equality and believed it to be their human right, not just a privilege bestowed by whites in power. And therein lay the tension between Granddaddy and how the younger generation of his sons viewed their existence in the Jim Crow South. Most of his boys wouldn't call white men "Boss" or feel allegiance to Alabama as their forever home, not like Granddaddy did.

Understand that the Page family had straddled the borders of Dallas and Perry Counties at least since Prince Page was born there sometime between 1837 and 1840. (No one can be sure of the precise birth date since people didn't bother to keep good records of Negroes or slaves back then.) Prince's mother and father came from Virginia, the first place many slaves touched American soil after those horrifying voyages from Africa. Slave owners often bought slaves at auctions in Virginia and transported them to lower southern states, including Alabama. If Prince's parents and he, as well, were slaves, they didn't count as whole people in those days, just three-fifths of a human for their masters' tax purposes.

Then came the Civil War, the Emancipation Proclamation, and freedom. Prince and his wife, Martha, had at least five children, likely the family's first to be born free on American soil. One son, they named Israel—Granddaddy's father. It only made sense to tell him how things used to be. How slave masters auctioned and sold them like cattle. How the industry stripped families apart, selling off daughters and sons to high bidders, never to see their parents or siblings again. Then Israel Sr. married a woman named Emma, and they had Israel Jr. in 1908. Like their parents before them, they told my grandfather about the culture of slavery, either directly or through their actions.

Granddaddy could've taken the antiwhite route, recalling all the wrongs done to him and the Pages before him. But he leaned softly when it came to whites and racism and human rights. Didn't worry much about making things different or asserting his manhood in uneasy situations, likely because he didn't imagine it would make a difference. "How you doing, Boss?" he said when passing a white man uptown.

His firstborn son, Dave Page, might be considered his opposite, at least when it came to reckoning discrimination with his rightful place in the world. Dave, on one extreme, held the superlatives among the Page children. The oldest, the best dressed, and most of all the bravest—or the craziest, depending on whom you ask. His life path meandered, and he moved to Brooksville, Florida, long before the events of this story. Family describe Granddaddy as laid-back, and white people called him a "good Negro." He greeted white people kindly, tipping his hat out of respect. For some, he'd likely been on their property, drilled their wells. Plus, he carried the title of a preacher, so people expected good, nonconfrontational behavior. For the most part, he lived up to it, avoiding much trouble in his life—legal, social, or otherwise.

But Dave?

"That Dave was something else," one of my uncles said.

"Dave was crazy," said another.

Uncle Howard explained with details and examples. "See, Dave was scared of nobody, white or Black," he said. "Me and Dave worked for the same man, now, and Dave wouldn't take no mess off of him. Dave would cuss [around] him just like he would anybody else."

Dave spent his childhood working cotton fields, so he couldn't read or write. Still, he didn't think much of white people who could; nor did he care what they thought of him. He worked hard, and when it was time to party, he slipped on his slacks, suit jacket, and matching dress shoes. "Sharp as a tack!" they say. No white man could convince Dave Page he wasn't good enough. To some, that was brave. To others, it seemed downright insane.

One day, for instance, he and Howard were working for a particular land-owner, plowing and picking, doing whatever the man asked, so they could get paid. Over walked the farmer's young daughter, and he introduced her to the Negro farmhands. For the purpose of this story, we'll call her Emily.

"Boys," he said, "this is my daughter, Miss Emily."

The way he said it, putting emphasis on the "Miss," let Dave and Howard know he expected the Negroes to address the boss's white daughter with re-spect, "Miss Emily." One problem: Dave was a grown man by then. He did not use courtesy titles for children standing at his hip. Besides, he was crazy. I can see Dave offering the boss and his daughter a tight little grin just for the fun of it.

Then, he said, "Hey there, Emily."

Dave went right back to doing what he was doing before little Emily showed up, like nothing had just happened. Howard stood there, silent, sneaking a peek at that white man and trembling a little inside. Back then, a Negro man could be beaten or killed for much less than Dave's blatant disregard, especially involving a white girl. And for whatever reason, Howard said, that white man did absolutely nothing about it. Of course, incidents like these only bolstered Dave's will to rebel against oppression, at least to the extent that he could and continue living.

Dave let people know his boundaries and held tight to pride in his own way. Had he been born a few decades later in Chicago or Oakland, California, he might have pumped his fist and chanted, "Power to the people," with the Black Panther Party. If alive today in his young manhood, I see him posting Facebook

Dave Page was known for his sharp
dressing and his boldness. *Page family
photo*

rants with the hashtag #BlackLivesMatter. I see him marching and protesting
and hoisting signs high. I see him demanding justice for the deaths of George
Floyd, Breonna Taylor, and Ahmaud Arbery, whose killings at the hands of
white men played into the ongoing nationwide protests of 2020.

To the contrary, Granddaddy made his way with a mild, slow, and steady ap-
proach. If he could get a hold of a newspaper, I see him reading stories about cy-
cles of racial unrest in America throughout the years. I see him using examples
of police brutality as talking points in his sermons, then asking believers to put
their faith in God. Around town, people knew Preacher Page because they'd

heard him preach. Or they'd played with him in the fields or darted alongside him through the woods as boys. They stopped and talked to him along the road. They nodded when he passed them in stores uptown and tipped his hat.

He focused on his family and getting by. But it took more than the widow's-mite-size offerings he got from church members or the small share from cotton-picking to support all those children, so Granddaddy kept his well-drilling job with Mr. Radford. Not that he didn't take pride in that, too. He did. He'd become good at it, testing grains of earth between his fingertips, directing workers on how to get the best results. He enjoyed getting in his old Chevy, going to work, and earning a decent check. I think he liked just being around the Radfords, too. He liked crossing the color line in fellowship, sitting together at their breakfast table, eating sunny-side-up eggs, the yolk runny and warm.

Before he moved away to Brooksville with Dave, my uncle Howard went along on some of Granddaddy's jobs. That is, when he wasn't planting, building, or doing other odd jobs. "White folks had big plantations, so I worked for them," he said. With Granddaddy, he gained a broader view of the area, beyond the backroads where he grew up. "We used to go all around to different houses," he recalled. They drove the land together, scoped the properties, and prepped them for new wells.

Most days, Granddaddy left for a job sometime in the morning and returned around sundown. The children were drained from picking cotton in the fields by then. He came in the house, pulling on his suspenders and wondering what Big Mama had cooked for all of them to eat—a routine not unlike the flow of life today. Then came July 15, 1954.

At the same time Granddaddy made his way along Highway 80 that morning, a white man named Brantley "B. B." Lee traveled to fulfill an assignment of his own. He had to transport a so-called crazy Negro from Talladega to the mental institution in Mount Vernon. Talladega was about 120 miles northwest of Browns, and the trip from there to Mount Vernon would be 250 miles. Besides the inmate, the deputy took some company along for the ride, including his brother and brother-in-law, for a total of four people in his cruiser that day.

About three hours in, Lee neared the end of a stretch south along State Road 5 where it intersected with Highway 80. Five being the smaller road, a stop sign warned drivers to halt and make sure the way was clear before crossing or turning onto 80. But Lee must've gotten distracted, perhaps talking with the others in the car; at least that's a logical guess. What's certain is that he did not stop, and his life tangled with Granddaddy's in such a way that the mess would never be undone.

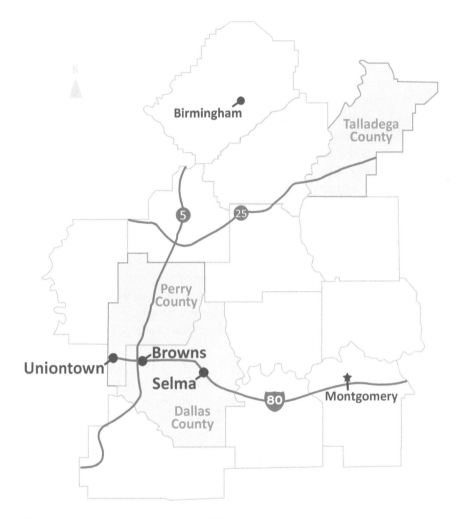

The Page family lived in the Browns and Uniontown area, near Selma, Alabama. Highway 80 was a major artery for travel and the site of a car accident that changed the Page family forever. *Aaron Robles, designer*

Lee crashed his cruiser into the side of Granddaddy's Chevy that day. The cruiser skidded ninety-six feet, then spun all around till it came to a stop in the opposite direction. Granddaddy's car went skidding along, too, finally resting sixty-nine feet away from the point of impact. The crash dented the Chevy's driver side and crushed the cruiser's nose. An ambulance showed up not too long after the spinning and burning rubber stopped. Deputy Lee's brother, Samuel S. Lee, suffered a broken leg and fractured ribs, while his brother-in-law got a few bruises. Deputy Lee, himself, got cut on his right ear and bruised on his face and hand. The mental patient, however, walked away with not a blemish to show for it. Ambulance workers checked the others and drove them to Vaughan Memorial Hospital in Selma.

Granddaddy took a direct hit. He bumped his head and went unconscious. When he came out of it, he couldn't move his right arm or hand. The hand that reached to grab hot biscuits in the morning and hard candies from his pocket for the kids. The hand he used to work the machine that drilled down into the earth's soil. The hand that reached down and scooped sand and tested the granules with his fingertips.

Highway patrolmen investigated. They noted the stop sign on State Road 5 where Deputy Lee came from, measured the skid marks, took statements from the deputy's passengers, and figured how the whole thing happened. Patrolman L. H. Hudson and his partner would later write their report. Meanwhile, officials dispatched someone else from Talladega to drive down and finish taking the inmate to Mount Vernon. Before leaving, that "insane Negro" told highway patrolmen exactly how he saw it.

"They are taking me to Mount Vernon because I'm crazy," he said to Hudson. "But I've got sense enough not to run that stop sign."

CHAPTER FOUR

—⚏—

MIGRATING TO A NEW LIFE

GRANDDADDY'S ACCIDENT took me on a journey, to discover not just the truth of his story but the essence of my own. How did the struggles that Negroes faced in the mid-twentieth century segue to my own battles as an African American woman in modern America? To answer that question, of course, I had to look one generation away to the link between myself and my grandparents: my own parents. In exploring Granddaddy's story, I realized how little I knew about our generational passage from the South to the Midwest.

My father came of age in Greensboro, Alabama. He accepted country living for what it was and held no aspirations for city life, until he started hearing folks talk of gainful employment up north. He'd worked various jobs since he could remember, helping his father and mother support a household of nine siblings. My paternal grandfather, Ullman Tubbs Sr., served in World War I and saved about $800 from his military pay to buy forty acres of farmland. The family grew corn to grind, make meal, and feed cows. He raised cotton and used the money from sales to buy more food. My father worked away from the house to buy school clothes and to cover other expenses.

The forty acres my grandfather bought had to mean a lot to him. He was born in 1888, not long after the Reconstruction era that really didn't reconstruct Negroes' lives much. The government had promised forty acres and a mule to help them recover economically and socially from slavery, but those promises blew away like chaff in the wind. Instead, domestic terrorism flourished through hate groups like the Klan, and oppression continued. In my spirit, I feel the pride that my father's father must've felt the day he paid for his own forty acres, land that would stay in the family for years to come. During our trips down south,

Ullman Tubbs Sr. and Mattie Tubbs with three of their older children (date unknown). *Tubbs family photo*

my father always took us to Greensboro after stopping at Big Mama's house. We visited my uncles and his mother, Mattie Tubbs, a petite woman with wavy hair and biracial features stemming partially from her Native American heritage. We all lovingly called her Fat Ma. The Tubbs family shack sat off a winding road, on land with greenery and tall trees that stretched until the treetops blended with the sky.

When we arrived for our summer visit, we usually saw Ullman Jr. (known as Uncle El) first, sitting on the porch, smiling as our car made its final turn up the road. He equipped himself with junk food snacks, cinnamon buns, chips, and generic strawberry and grape sodas. We'd sit for an hour or so, talking with El about school and boys or whatever, gently swaying on the porch swing that my father had made years earlier using steel chains and sturdy wooden slats. As we prepared to leave, Uncle El always reached into his pocket and gave us a dollar or two to enjoy and buy our own snacks. Sometimes, he mailed letters to us, tucking a few dollars inside for high school graduations and such, a major sacrifice for a country man in backwoods Alabama.

Ullman Tubbs Sr. bought forty acres of land, after saving money from his service in
World War I. *Sharon Tubbs photo*

But long before all this, back in August 1959, Uncle El found his father lying
on the ground near the woods. He'd had a stroke. The military paid a taxi driver
$31 to take him to a veteran's hospital in Tuskegee, 150 miles away. That was big
money back then, and my father recalled the details. He and Fat Ma rode with
my grandfather in the taxi. They got him all the way there for help, but he never
recovered. He died at the hospital just shy of his seventy-first birthday.

My father emerged as the head of the household, overseeing the family farm
and sawing down trees in the Alabama woods. He and a small crew cut the tree
trunks into smaller logs, loaded them onto trucks, and transported the wood
to companies that made paper. The work proved hard and dangerous. Not long
before he started, a man doing the same work died when a tree toppled over
and crushed him. Still, it yielded about forty dollars a week—"pretty good pay,"
my father said, when you could get it. Seasonal rain and cold made the work
temperamental at best.

A door opened for better in May 1963. One of his older sisters had married a
man who settled up north. My father rode with her and her small children on

a one-way bus trip to Fort Wayne, Indiana. He tagged along to help my aunt with her kids on the trip and to reunite her family. He worked it out with my aunt and her husband so that he would get to stay. He'd live with them until he made enough money to get a place of his own. He was twenty-three years old.

"I figured I could probably get a better job, coming up here," he said.

Soon he landed steady work at Mike's Carwash, an upgrade. "Well, better than cutting logs out in the woods," he said, "but it didn't take much to get better than that."

He hoped for more. Like others, he migrated with a plan to work for one of the big northern factories. In Fort Wayne, Blacks and whites wore goggles and work gloves inside plants for Dana, GTE, Zollner Piston, and International Harvester, the once-powerful national manufacturer of auto and farm equipment. At one time, Harvester stood among the city's largest employers.

"While you worked at the car wash, you'd be looking for a good job, like at the Harvester," my father said. "You get a job at the Harvester, you'd be something, or at Zollner, Piston. Those were good factory jobs."

Somewhere between the drive for factory work and a better life, Black migrants found opportunities for a good time, too. One Saturday night in late October, five months after landing in Fort Wayne, my father was hanging out at a bar with his brother-in-law and some coworkers from the carwash. Someone mentioned a house party nearby on Masterson Street, and they made their way over. Three women, cousins, were hosting the gathering. Each wore the same black sheath dress, so they'd stand out to their guests. The modest crowd mingled in the house basement, many of them transplants from down south. They chatted in small groups about which county or city or rural area they'd left for city life up north. The sounds of guitars and the beat of drums drifted from blues music on the record player.

The night wore on, and my father realized he hadn't talked to one of the three hostesses, the shortest one in the black sheath. Imagine him, beckoning her to come where he stood. He asks her name.

"Julia," she tells him. "Julia Page."

He tells her his name, and they make small talk about the party and such. He asks the question Blacks in Indiana often did since, more than likely, they both had migrated to the area.

"Where're your people from?"

Scholars later put facts and figures behind what Blacks like my father saw with their eyes. So many Blacks drifted northward during the early twentieth century that by 1970 most African Americans lived outside of the South for the first time in American history. When it came to Blacks from those southern central states—Alabama, Mississippi, Kentucky, and Tennessee—75 percent got on the nearest highway or train line and journeyed straight up, landing in the Midwest. They came as much for economic opportunity as they did to escape the racist South.

"Uniontown, Alabama," she tells him, "over in Perry County." (By the time my mother moved to Indiana, the Pages had moved the short distance from Browns to Uniontown.)

My father nods because he knows Uniontown, since it's not too far south from his stomping grounds, about twenty miles from Greensboro. They talk about their lives in this new land where dirt is a deep brown, houses stand close together, and kids walk on sidewalks.

She migrated the same year, earlier that summer. Her brothers already lived in Indiana and figured the North to be a better environment for a young twenty-year-old woman to make a way for herself. Julia and her cousins rented rooms on the second floor of this house on Masterson Street, while her older cousin and his wife lived on the first floor. She found a quick job at Slick's Laundry, ironing shirts and slacks for white folks who could afford to pay somebody else to handle their clothes. Down south, she'd ironed and starched for her brothers, not to mention the bed sheets and Big Mama's good bedspreads, too. (Down south, some bedrooms transitioned to sitting rooms during the day, so they made the beds each morning, and Big Mama liked her sheets neat, clean, and crisp.) Here, at least Mama got paid for it, and she didn't have to spend hours in that hot cotton field on top of it.

Later that night, a small melee distracted everybody from the fun. It started, as my father recalls, when one man punched a tipsy man who was talking trash. The party ended, and all the visitors got kicked out. The car wash crew and a couple of others weren't ready to go home, though. They pitched ideas to keep their personal party rolling, then divided into two cars and headed east toward Lima, Ohio, where nightclubs awaited. My father settled in one car with his brother-in-law and another man. Three friends from the car wash rode in the other car. But about twenty minutes into their trip, tragedy ended it all on Highway 30. The other car, with the three car wash friends, veered into oncoming traffic on a two-lane bridge. It crashed head-on with a semitruck.

My father saw the car flip in front of him, watched it spiral into the night. One passenger's body pounded the hood of the car with my father inside. The other bodies landed elsewhere. All three men in the crashed car died. The semitruck driver suffered only minor bruises. My father and his brother-in-law talked to authorities, then left the scene unharmed, at least not physically wounded.

John and Julia Tubbs, early 1960s. *Tubbs family photo*

Of course, the experience stuck with them. Three of my father's cowork-ers—the men he laughed with while waxing car hoods, the ones he partied with on weekends—were gone in an instant. Who could forget "Big Wine," as they called the one, speculated to have an affinity for the spirits? Another had a wife and several children. He'd just bought a new car, the one that crashed. All three men were migrants, too, originally from Alabama, Tennessee, and Mississippi.

The next day, my father needed someone to talk to about all that had hap-pened, someone besides his brother-in-law and sister. He remembered the short woman in the black sheath at the party. They had chatted easily and seemed to have a lot in common, them both being from the same region in Alabama. He borrowed his brother-in-law's car and drove back to Masterson Street. Four-teen months later, John Tubbs and Julia Page said wedding vows, and the family grew. My parents each had children from previous relationships who lived with Granddaddy and Big Mama and a loved one in Alabama, before having children together. All told, I was the youngest of seven.

Daddy left Mike's Carwash after a while and landed jobs driving taxis and stocking groceries, until he finally got on at Lincoln Foodservice, a factory where workers assembled industrial cooking equipment. The annual company party for employees and their families ranged from bland chicken banquets to picnics with hot dogs. For years, my father rose too early for us to see him before school, the kind of man who arrived in time to get settled and talk and drink coffee before the labor began. He never missed work. One of his proudest moments each year came when Lincoln handed out cash bonuses for workers with perfect attendance. He'd come home and tell us all about it, flipping through the extra bills in his wallet.

Meanwhile, Mama left Slick's Laundry for a job with the state of Indiana. She worked at an institution that housed and cared for people with developmental disabilities. Mama worked the second shift, so she could make sure my brother, sister, and I got ready for school. By the time we came back home, she'd already have left for work. She hid the housekey someplace on the porch for me to get inside and left dinner in pots and pans on the stove.

Summertime meant a visit to see our grandparents in Alabama, which my parents called home but my generation called "down south." We'd pile into our green Bonneville and later the gray Buick with the maroon top. We wedged our mismatched suitcases into the trunk around a cooler full of Faygo pops, orange and grape and lemon lime, that came five for a dollar. The youngest and the skinniest, I squeezed into the middle, between my brother and sister, my butt bumping against the middle hump in the back seat. I rode wide-eyed the whole twelve hours, fighting sleep through Kentucky and the mountains of Tennessee, up and down the rollercoaster red hills of northern Alabama.

We'd stop at gas stations along Interstate 69 to fill up, use the restroom, and buy salty peanuts, Baby Ruths, Snickers bars, pork rinds, and Funyuns. We ate McDonald's cheeseburgers and fries and sang along to "Double Dutch Bus." We listened to my father's bass boom in sync with squealing guitars and gritty blues classics on eight tracks. We snickered and soaked in lyrics to "Wang Dang Doodle," "Clean Up Woman," and even "Hoochie Coochie Man."

"You need to turn that mess off!" Mama would say.

Daddy just laughed it off and kept singing: "We gonna wang dang doodle, all night long!"

Jim Crow seemed so far away from our life in the Midwest, at least in my childhood mind. He lived on the pages of my school history books, not in our homes, not on our road trips, not in our conversations on country porch swings. In reality, the racism and segregation he symbolized spread like a virus from the South to the North and all parts in between.

Laughter and dancing were a big part of family gatherings. Here, John and Julia do a dance called "the bump." *Tubbs family photo*

When my parents married in 1965, a few white neighbors lived near their first place, including a particularly nosy lady who peeked out the window whenever visitors drove up to the house. Their second house sat next door to a white man who eventually sold his slice of land and moved away. My father bought it and planted a crabapple tree. The white neighbors joined others in their exodus, leaving city cores for neighborhoods on the outskirts and across the railroad tracks of Fort Wayne. Nationwide, redlining cemented segregation, as white realtors, builders, finance companies, and even government agencies drew boundaries around certain inner-city areas and steered Blacks there. Meanwhile, they designated and financed land in the suburbs and on the outskirts for whites, although some Black people of means eventually scattered among them. In my earliest memories, east central Fort Wayne, where we lived, equaled a bona fide chocolate city. My parents had moved a couple times during the early years of their marriage but stayed in the same vicinity. For every Black migrant from the South who moved into the area, two whites moved out to the suburbs, for reasons that likely included economic factors and racial prejudice, too, according to the Princeton University economist Leah Platt Boustan.

Fort Wayne's factories brought the colors together for the sake of earning a living. Throughout the North, white supervisors constrained Black factory workers to lower-paying or undesirable jobs. The dynamic created competition within the labor market between southern migrants and Blacks who already lived in the North, Platt Boustan says. They fought among themselves for limited positions. In theory, some didn't have the education for higher-level positions due to the quality of some segregated schools in the South. Whites decided Blacks were educationally inferior, then fulfilled their own prophecy by offering substandard education systems, if any at all. Then again, some employers were just racist anyway and set aside all the desirable positions for white laborers.

The schools also joined Black, brown, and white kids together. A set of railroad tracks along the Maumee River literally separated the neighborhood where my family lived from middle-class whites on the tracks' other side. Over there, white kids took pride in calling themselves "Hoosiers," because their parents were Indiana natives. We didn't understand or really care what the word *Hoosiers* meant. Buses transported these different perspectives and cultures to school buildings and on field trips, like adventures to the zoo or the Historic Old Fort, a replica of a fort constructed in the early nineteenth century for defense against Native Americans.

By the time I attended Lakeside Middle School, the city had funded a busing system that carried me a little more than a mile away to start the day. My older brother and his friends experienced a much different journey to the classroom, several years earlier. Buses didn't stop in our neighborhood back then, so they walked across the tracks. The distance proved no problem, but the transition of worlds did. A group of white high school boys got a kick out of terrorizing them along the way. "Porch monkeys!" they called out from their yards or their car windows. The white teens gave chase at times, their longer legs tracking down the elementary and middle schoolers. My brother Arbra scurried through yards and alleyways, trying to ditch his would-be attackers. He always did, but they caught one of his friends once. "He got beat pretty bad," Arbra said. Other times, a teen driving a black Dodge Charger trailed them through residential streets. Whenever they saw the Charger, they dodged to an escape route. Equally interesting for me, my brother had not shared these stories until I asked him as an adult if he experienced racism growing up. He'd accepted this routine of Black kids running from white kids as a norm, his lot as a youth in Fort Wayne during the seventies. At the time, the whole thing felt like a corrupt childhood "adventure," he said.

Halloween changed the game, though. Every year, on October 31, Blacks could walk on the other side of the tracks without being chased, at least not openly. Few porch lights lit up in my neighborhood to welcome trick-or-treaters. Families directly across the street and around the corner also were migrants, so our parents rarely spent hard-earned factory money on elaborate Halloween costumes. I recall a few times when my father bought bags of candy to hand out and turned on the porch light, but he got very few trick-or-treaters in our neighborhood since participating houses were few and far between.

I'd grab one of my mother's old shopping bags and cross the tracks with my big sister and other neighborhood kids, most of us donning cheap plastic masks chosen hastily from clearance racks at Walgreens. I recall wearing what I figured must be a King Kong mask, despite having no affinity for the character whatsoever. In fact, I wore that mask two or three years in a row. It served its purpose, helping me curry favor at well-to-do households where homeowners seemed less generous with mask-less kids. "Where's *your* mask?" they'd ask. If we wanted candy, we had to take this holiday seriously, or at least look like we did.

Hoosiers on the other side of the tracks had money for Dodge Chargers and good candy, too. That much we could tell when driving by on our way to the grocery store or the mall, seeing their yards saturated with lights, scarecrows, skeletons, and other displays of spookiness and frivolity. They could afford mini Snickers bars and Reese's peanut butter cups, not to mention the high electric bills. Their kids wore full-body costumes, some hand-sewn, their cheeks beaming with painted-on whiskers or the blush of a little princess.

These displays of lavishness with money and time marked the "white life," I figured, since they echoed story lines seen on mainstream TV. Their lifestyles equaled the stuff of *Three's Company* or *Brady Bunch*, while ours resembled more of a *Good Times* narrative. My father substituted for James Evans, working hard every day at the factory. But unlike his TV wife, my mother and most of the women I knew worked outside the home. In addition to her job at the state institution, she sometimes picked up a second job as a caregiver, cooking and cleaning for the elderly or the disabled in their homes.

Once, Mama refused to care for a client, after the mean old lady ordered her around, talking down to her like a new-age slave, even called her a nigger. Mama drew on the spirit of Big Mama and her brother Dave that day. She called her boss on the client's phone, while the bed-bound woman watched and couldn't do a thing about it. Mama told the supervisor what had happened, picked up her purse, and walked right out the door. At home later, she shared the story with us, emphasizing that we didn't have to put up with such degrading treatment, not in these days.

Two working parents in the home made me different from some classmates. Our family wages couldn't buy me or my siblings a car for our sixteenth birthdays, but we didn't qualify for free lunch either, and my father was proud of that, just as proud as his own father had felt buying land to provide for their family. My father cashed his checks on Fridays, and he'd call us all together, as he took out his wallet. His fingers flipped through bills still crisp from the bank, and he doled out our allowance and lunch money one by one. I'd fold those dollar bills and tuck them safely away on top of my bedroom dresser to buy lunch and snacks the following week.

People say socioeconomic status is generational. Growing up, I didn't think about our status much. We never went hungry or lived outdoors, so all seemed well in my eyes. I know now that there were times we lived only a smidgen above "just getting by," and I can see that status and work ethic running generationally through our family stories, perhaps through our very veins. One grandfather bought his own land, enough to secure the family a place to live, while they still labored to buy school clothes, food, and other basic needs that did not come easily. The other grandfather sharecropped and drilled wells to provide just enough—until the day came when he no longer could.

CHAPTER FIVE

GETTING RELIGION

THE DAY GRANDDADDY'S ACCIDENT happened, hours passed before Big Mama got to the hospital. A family friend with a car gave her a ride, along with Willie James and Robert Lee. The younger kids could mind the house till they all got back. When they arrived, Granddaddy lay on a cot, wearing the same clothes from that morning, now stained with dried blood. No one had tended to his head injuries or shattered arm.

"When we walked in, he started crying, and he was just lying there," Willie James said. No one had given him a pill or medicine for the pain.

A newspaper article about the accident mentioned Granddaddy at Burwell Infirmary, a small, segregated nursing home and sometime-hospital with Negro doctors and nurses. In many public hospitals, white doctors wouldn't work with Negro doctors, and they sometimes shuffled Black patients down to basements for substandard treatment. The blatant discrimination drove Black health professionals to join with philanthropic organizations from the North and such religious institutions as the Catholic Church to create their own hospitals in what became known as the Black Hospital Movement.

Beginning in the 1800s, these separate hospitals gave aspiring Black medical professionals a chance to treat patients and hone their skills. But just like segregated Black schools of that era, the facilities lagged their counterparts due to inferior equipment or lack of it, strained staff from too many patients, and not enough trained doctors and nurses to go around.

If an ambulance took Granddaddy to Burwell initially, like the newspaper said, someone later transported him to the main area hospital, Vaughan Memorial. He eventually underwent surgery at Vaughan. Willie James saw white

35

nurses and sensed prejudice when Big Mama and the boys arrived, so Granddaddy may have been at Vaughan by then. After the tears dried, Granddaddy told what happened as best he could, considering the pain. While he talked, Willie James noticed the staff didn't seem anxious to help. Later that evening, he overheard one nurse tell another, "Somebody should see about that Negro on the cot."

"They probably didn't care if he died or not," he figured.

A doctor later examined Granddaddy and determined he had a broken arm, a crushed ulna, and a damaged radial nerve. The injuries meant possibly losing his arm. Granddaddy would endure a two-week hospital stay at some point. Big Mama visited when she could get a ride, like the time Granddaddy's brother, Uncle White, drove down from Birmingham and picked her up. He brought along Granddaddy's older daughters, who'd moved away from home by then. They offered comforting words and prayers Granddaddy needed to hear. Everyone realized the high stakes by now. Sharecropping and drilling wells were the steady-paying jobs Granddaddy had for his entire adult life. Without that arm, he could not drill wells for Cecil Radford, and the family would lose their main source of income.

The day after the accident, a story in the *Selma Times-Journal* told what happened. The headline read, "Three Injured in Crash at Browns: Crash First of Year at Intersection."

> The first 1954 traffic mishap at the Browns intersection of U.S.
> Highway 80 and Alabama Five hospitalized three persons Thursday, one
> of whom suffered a broken leg and rib fractures.
>
> The Highway Patrol reported that two autos, one of which was being
> driven by a Talladega County deputy sheriff who was carrying an insane
> Negro to Mt. Vernon, ran together at the crossing near noon. . . .
>
> Israel Page, 46, a Browns Negro, was named as the driver and
> only occupant of the other auto involved. He suffered a fracture of the
> right arm and is being treated at the Burwell Infirmary.
>
> Patrolmen L. H. Hudson, W. H. Wells and J. R. Vanderford, who
> investigated, blamed the collision on the deputy sheriff for his failure to
> halt at the intersection.

Through the ordeal, Granddaddy's faith stepped to the forefront. It had to, beckoning him and the whole family to lean in and believe, in spite of the struggle ahead. In my mind, this struggle, or one like it, was inevitable. Granddaddy's very name alluded to it. In the Bible, God gave men names with meanings that revealed something about them. That's as good a reason as any for a man to be named Israel, a word that some scholars translate to mean "he struggles with God." Jacob wrestled with an angel yet overcame the fight, and God changed his name to Israel. No angelic force descended from the heavens for a miraculous duel with Granddaddy, but for a Negro born in 1908 to be called Israel, the Lord must have had something in mind. Since Granddaddy's father was an Israel, too, I imagine the Pages had struggled for a while. And that's saying something, because carving out life in those backwoods could make it hard to tell the difference between struggling and not struggling. Backbreaking work greeted them with the sun and only walked away when it set. What outsiders called hard, they called easy, and what strangers called easy, they called blessed.

That's what looking at life through the lens of faith could do. Faith offered a future that played out far differently than their current situation suggested it would. At that hospital, the family looked down at Granddaddy's crushed arm and saw how the nurses ignored his pain. Yet faith gave hope for a good outcome—at least as good as this world could muster for a Negro. Big Mama used to sing a song that fit the narrative of slaves working and singing in the fields. Masters routinely beat or sold away their loved ones, tearing mothers, fathers, and siblings apart. The song's origins are unclear, but some form of the lyrics still resonate because my mother sang them occasionally while cooking in the kitchen. It is a slow hymn, in rich, solemn tones.

> This world is a mean world to live in, try to stay here, till you die.
> No mother, no father. No sister, and you got no brother.
> This world is a mean world to live in, try to stay here, till you die.
> Sometimes, you got to fall on your knees to live here, try to stay here,
>   till you die.

As mean as this world felt for Negroes, Granddaddy and Big Mama figured faith could get them through it. They considered faith to feed the soul as important as food to feed the body. The Page children had to believe in the core of the Christian faith: that Jesus Christ died for their sins and rose again. When someone confesses this belief today, Protestants call it "getting saved," but they called it "getting religion" back then. It was a process. Some people say salvation is free, but in the Page house, that didn't mean it came easily.

"It was a Wednesday night when I came through," my mother told me. "When he was preaching, seemed like there was a blaze of fire. Next thing I know I was running down the aisle."

Picture the middle of the annual summer revival at St. Mary's church, mid-1950s. Granddaddy preached at El Bethel and Little Union, but, come July, the different Negro congregations in the area, hungry for a special message from the Lord, gathered together for revival at St. Mary's. This particular summer, a guest minister came from Birmingham to lead services. And if anybody could preach, they say that man sure could.

Church leaders reserved a pew up front as the "mourning bench" (or "mourner's bench") for youth who wanted to get religion that year. Age thirteen, Mama sat in that row, waiting for a divine touch from the Lord. By then, she'd been praying and fasting for two or three days, typical for those on the bench. Revival gave God a week to reach young souls like hers, at least those open wide enough to receive him. Candidates held their heads down, asking God to move. They prayed for forgiveness. They prayed that the stain of sin be washed clean. They cried and tarried for the Holy Ghost power to show up.

While the young folks prayed and waited on God, Big Mama sat at the front of the church, watching and waiting, too, her eyes fixed on them. She watched much closer than Granddaddy and probably just a blink or two less than the Holy Ghost. Officially speaking, Granddaddy stood as the head and preacher of the family, but Big Mama was the enforcer when it came to everything from chores to curfews, dating, and getting religion, too. Every year, come revival season, one or two of the kids professed that their time had come. Big Mama didn't debate them. She just let them go and sit on the bench. Then she watched, watched for signs of the Spirit at work. That typically meant streaming tears, an uncontrollable shout, a jerk from a divine tingle down the spine, or something else that couldn't be faked or performed for show.

When the service ended each night, the candidates went home and prayed some more.

"You didn't go to bed some nights," my mother said. "You'd sit out on the porch till daybreak, praying and asking, 'God if you heard my prayer, let me hear the dove moan.' And eventually you'd hear it moan," Mama said.

Amid the fasting, praying, and moaning doves, my mother's heart ripened for conversion into the kingdom of God. We don't know exactly what that guest preacher said, but whatever it was, it hit Mama like a lightning bolt, had her jumping up and running through that church like somebody was chasing her.

"They say Uncle Scoe caught me, 'cause I was running," she said. After that, she calmed and came to herself. "I was walking down the aisle, talking about my religion"—a sign she'd gone dead to her old sinful ways and joined other Christians promised eternal life.

"So glad I died," she sang that night. "Ain't gonna die no more."

After conversion, my mother walked from house to house, telling people about God, about how he died on the cross, how he washed away her sins, how he saved her. Granddaddy baptized her later that summer in a pond just beyond Little Union. She wore a white gown with a cap on her head. She walked

Robert Lee Paige. *Page family photo*

barefoot while family and church members ringed the pond, singing, "Take me to the water."

Thank goodness she got religion that time since it was her second attempt. During the prior year's revival, my mother sat on the bench night after night, but her spine tingled not. Her eyes didn't sting with tears. She could only watch as others crossed over, jumping and crying out. Tired of seeing everybody else get it, Mama bowed her head, licked her finger, and rubbed the spit on her cheeks to look like tears. Making matters worse, she had already cheated a little on her fasting vow, and Robert Lee offered no mercy. "I can tell you ain't really doing nothing," he'd told her one day. "You eating too much."

The revival continued, and Robert Lee wouldn't let up. The final dig came when Big Mama made sticky rolls, a special sweet family treat. He got a warm, fresh roll and savored it right in my mother's twelve-year-old face. She succumbed to temptation and got one of her own, effectively breaking her fast and ending her bid for religion that year.

Mama wasn't the only one who required two rounds on the bench, though. Indeed, some Page kids who declared they'd gotten religion couldn't satisfy Big Mama's discernment for authenticity. "You ain't got nothing," she'd say. "Go on back." They returned to the bench to pray harder or longer, because if Big Mama didn't deem it to be real, it wasn't.

Robert Lee, himself, knew the feeling, which might be why he sabotaged my mother. His first go-round, Big Mama didn't see enough reform in his mischievous spirit—and much mischief there was. Mind you, Robert Lee was the son known for sneaking into his uncle's house to steal hoecakes off the stove, which he dumped into a creek just for the fun of it. He was the one who pulled off the most peculiar heist in Page history when he snuck and picked cotton from a neighbor's field. Then, pretending he'd picked it elsewhere, Robert Lee knocked on that same neighbor's door later with a bold pitch to sell the man's own cotton back to him.

Yes, Big Mama would have to see strong, clear evidence that Robert Lee crossed over to the Lord's side. The first time he hopped up, claiming a good feeling, she called him out. "Boy, you ain't got nothing. Go on back!" His response is now the stuff of family legend: "Well, see, I had it," he told her. "But soon as I got 'round that there corner, the devil took it from me!" Robert Lee went back to the bench, and at some point, he stopped playing games. The Spirit wrested his soul good, to the point where even Big Mama couldn't deny it.

Similar scenes played out with Willie James, whose first attempt fell short. "Go on back," Big Mama told him.

But Willie James refused—at least that summer. He waited a whole year, for the next revival season, before sitting on the bench again. Some called him "stubborn" or "just a mean little thing" in his younger years. Whatever the description, when Willie James set his mind to something, he rarely backed down. He once held an ax to his sister Ossie Mae's throat. She'd cooked a batch of biscuits and clearly instructed him not to mess with them. Quite particular about the way his sisters cooked family meals, he refused to eat bread not sufficiently browned on the bottom to his liking. On this day, he went directly into the kitchen and inspected those biscuits. Ossie Mae caught him peeking, perhaps even taking a pinch off one to test its quality, and she told him a thing or two. Willie James grabbed an ax nearby and pinned her to the wall. She cried out for Granddaddy.

"You better come get him, before I hurt him!" she screamed.

"Hurt *him*?" Granddaddy said, in his usual pinched tone. "How you gon' hurt him, and he got you up against the wall with that ax?"

Willie James Page. *Page family photo*

Of course, Willie James turned her loose. And when it came to his second time on the mourning bench, the Spirit pinned him down, such that surrender was his only option. Big Mama approved. She knew that feeling of surrender to God's calling. Big Mama, herself, was said to have gotten religion at age twelve. If her conversion looked like others in that era, she felt so joyful on the inside that she couldn't keep quiet. She walked up and down the countryside, telling people about the Lord and about a better place for Negroes up in heaven. That desire to spread the Gospel stayed with her. She always talked about faith in times of trouble, telling people from one generation to the next what God could do.

As for Granddaddy, when his time for religion came, an old country preacher named Reverend Murray led him down to the water, dunked him, and proclaimed him to be "born again," by the Spirit. They say baptism is a public sign of an inner transformation, a new acceptance in the heart and mind that Jesus is the savior. Once Granddaddy came up from that water, everyone could tell he was walking with the Lord now.

Still, it surprised some when he later declared his claim to the pulpit. He'd been drilling wells since before he and Big Mama married, when he was nineteen and she was seventeen. As far as anybody could figure, the title of preacher skipped his list of callings, and he'd live out his days as a well driller and sharecropper. Granddaddy's youngest brother, Frank, remembered way back, back when he was a little boy and Granddaddy was a young adult. They'd be out in the fields, picking cotton, and Granddaddy would start talking like a Negro Baptist preacher, with that forceful tone and singsong storytelling style Negroes used to close out their sermons. They call it "whooping" or "hooping," depending on who's spelling it. Granddaddy would be picking and whooping, and Frank listened to his every word. It seemed like playfulness at the time. The family went to church, of course, but like a good deal of the young men back then, Granddaddy enjoyed a swig of whiskey too.

Then God came calling, in the same way he called other unlikely candidates to lead the people, like the stuttering Moses, the shy Timothy, or the gruff Peter. Nowadays, in fact, it seems many sitting in churches have a used-to-be story, so to speak. They used to be drug addicts, drug dealers, alcoholics, cheaters, and swindlers. They used to be promiscuous or homeless, prison inmates or party animals, whom no one ever thought would stumble into the kingdom, certainly not tripping all the way to the pulpit. Then, one day, some inkling they'd tucked far in the back of their beings, behind all the mess, they let that inkling rise up and be considered. That's when the door opened wide enough for God's voice to seep in and issue the calling.

"He always had a voice," Frank said, remembering those sermonettes between cuts of cotton. "He used to do that in the field."

When the stirring in his soul felt too clear to let it pass, Granddaddy told Big Mama that the Lord had called him.

"Well, if he called," she said, "I reckon you better go on and answer."

And he did.

People saw the pastoral calling with prestige and honor in those days, more so than they do today. A Negro preacher found dignity in the pulpit, despite finding disrespect elsewhere. The church stood as the core of the Black community. It had to, since white folks controlled everything else. No matter how much cussing, fighting, and fornicating went on at home, just about everybody went to church sometime. In the Lord's house, they could meet and celebrate. They could sing, dance, and even shout if they wanted. That's why a Black man back then couldn't get much higher than a preacher. A man of God could pray for the sick, marry the young, counsel the troubled, and usher the sinner man away from the gates of hell.

Granddaddy pastored several churches as his preaching status advanced, including El Bethel and Little Union. Churches didn't hold service every week, so sometimes Granddaddy presided over two churches at a time, rotating Sundays. At home, Big Mama lived out her role as the typical country wife, having babies at a pace of about one every two years. Rosie was the one whose spirit escaped to heaven not long after birth. The others grew up as Pages, with few, if any, making it out without sitting on that bench to get religion.

In all truth, questions of propriety occasionally arose, even in a church full of the Holy Ghost and a preacher called by God. Granddaddy and the family listened to more than weather and funeral notices on the radio, for instance. Once, a popular Ray Charles tune bellowed through the house. A rising star in Granddaddy's day, Charles mixed secular music and lyrics with traditional gospel arrangements. In his hit duet "Night Time Is the Right Time," Charles sang of desire to be with the woman he loved. A female vocalist cried out, "Baby!" pleading with her lover to hold her tight. "Baby! Baby! Baby! Oh, baby!" Surprisingly, Granddaddy held a fondness for it.

"That girl know she singing that song," he would say when he heard it.

My mother and aunt giggled. Despite its churchy rhythms, "Night Time" had nothing to do with religion, of course, and they thought the pastor's fondness for it funny. He obviously hadn't listened closely to the lyrics. Finally, they told him, "That's a blues song, Daddy."

Nonetheless, there are vague memories of a woman belting out her own version of the song during church one Sunday. It is said that she boldly, although not so cleverly, swapped the lyric "Baby!" for a call of comfort from the savior— "Jesus! Jesus! Jesus! Oh, Jesus!" We don't know how this all came about, but I would venture to say that, if true, Big Mama did not feel the Spirit.

Antics like these aside, the family took faith seriously. Granddaddy and Big Mama grew up in a time of lynching and cross burnings, and religion gave kids what they needed to survive. The world turned mean on Negroes, just like Big Mama sang. Without faith, without looking up to someone higher and better, the young ones wouldn't be able to keep on living, working, and thriving under that level of stress. They *had* to get religion, so they could cope if they ever got in an accident and lost a limb and a livelihood, all at the same time. They *had* to believe in God and learn how to fall on their knees. The struggles to come required nothing less.

CHAPTER SIX

—ᔇᔇ—

A DIFFERENT KIND OF SHOUT

AS FAR BACK as I can remember, Sunday mornings were made for church, and Granddaddy's "thousand-dollar girl" took me and my siblings to the Lord's house. I stood in stiff A-line dresses, singing and clapping right along with the morning's opening song at Jerusalem Baptist. The church nestled in southeast Fort Wayne, adorned with a stone and brick pattern on the outside and wooden pews on the inside. Sometimes the organ and drums accented our voices; other times we intoned a cappella. Lyrics flowed from my memory and through my lips. I didn't know what most of the songs really meant, at least not then, but I knew the words.

"Have you *got* good religion?" a deaconess at the front of the church sang.

We responded: "Certainly, Lord."

"Have you *got* good re-*li-gion*?"

"Certainly, Lord."

"Have you *got* good religion?"

"Certainly, Lo-*oord*! Certainly, certainly, certainly, Lord!"

My mother presided over the church's usher board, dutifully wearing a gold-plated badge pinned to the collar of a navy, off-white, gray, or black suit. She and her team in matching suits sat on the last pew in the back of the church, which provided a full view of any shenanigans occurring from the rear of the sanctuary to the choir loft behind the pulpit.

At times they marched the aisles in sync, one hand behind their backs, the other distributing paper fans to the overheated, handing out envelopes, or passing collection plates to gather the week's tithes and offerings. They stood at the double doors that separated the vestibule and the sanctuary to stop late-comers from entering during a sacred prayer. They gave antsy, loud-talking, gum-chewing children the evil eye or a good talking to. With Mama being the head usher for most of my childhood, I dutifully sat up straight without saying a word until the time came to sing.

Have you been baptized?

Certainly, Lord.

The pastor and his family were Alabama migrants like us. In fact, they'd lived not far from the Pages. The same was true of other families in the church. My aunts, my uncles and their wives or significant others, my cousins, my mother's cousins and their children—most of them attended Jerusalem Baptist, too. Sundays became a mini reunion of Alabama families originally from Perry and Dallas Counties. They drove hundreds of miles to cluster around some of the same folks they'd sat beside at a colored school in the South. Only now, they assembled in the pews at Jerusalem Baptist or Pilgrim Baptist, True Love, St. John, Union, or Progressive—some of the main predominantly Black Baptist churches in Fort Wayne. They journeyed here and found others they knew or would get to know from the South.

In my public school, teachers and city leaders publicized a sister city kinship with Takaoka, Japan. We did activities to learn about the people and the culture there. The suits at city hall didn't know it, but Fort Wayne had much deeper ties with what the author Isabel Wilkerson called our "sister cities" in the South. These were our native enclaves in rural Alabama, like Browns and Uniontown, not to mention coves in Mississippi, South Carolina, Louisiana, and Arkansas, from where groups of southerners followed brothers, cousins, and friends to Fort Wayne. During our summertime trips down south, our migrant families brought back foods scarce in Fort Wayne, like purple hull peas, hog headcheese, red hot sausage links, certain brands of self-rising corn meal, and fresh peanuts, walnuts, and pecans still in their shells. In church, we stood together, praising God.

These church services up north differed in some ways from the southern sanctuaries where many migrants had learned religion. For one thing, our parents used money from their factory and government jobs to buy wardrobes of suits and dresses, choir robes, and even instruments for the sanctuary. In rural Alabama at the time, many families couldn't afford multiple Sunday outfits, and they often kept the beat with the stomp of their feet on wood plank floors.

Still, our worship experiences in Fort Wayne clearly mingled the cultures from various sister cities in the South. I took in these traditions without knowing it. The generation before me experienced God amid constant segregation and prejudice. I can only imagine the sadness, grief, and all kinds of emotions stirred from such oppression and struggle. Our ancestors then carried that passion and intensity with them northbound to their migrant church circles.

For example, some often expressed joy and released pent-up sadness and frustration by "shouting"—and I don't mean a brief scream. Say "shouting" in the old Black Baptist or Pentecostal context, and it means much more than that. As best I can describe it, shouting amounted to an eruption of emotions that overflowed in a spiritual volcano of movement and sound. It could be an unction from the Spirit to get up and move about, to praise God openly. It could also be a way of laying down one's burdens, letting it all hang out. The practice took on myriad forms, some of them as unique as the person shouting in the moment. A happy shout, for instance, might look like someone standing up and doing a jig to the music, not like the modern dances we did to songs on the radio but more of a euphoric foot shuffle to the beat of the piano, organ, and drums as a show of praise to God. After all they'd been through, they rejoiced in survival.

The tradition goes at least as far back as slavery, possibly before it. Slaves dug up joy from someplace in their souls, gathered in circles, created their own beats, and took turns dancing in the center. This joy carried over from the slave fields to the church house decades later when Negroes thought of something to really praise God for. Every now and then, somebody at Jerusalem "got happy" or "caught the spirit," as they'd say, and danced in the aisles. Sometimes, the more radical, the better. Believers likened the practice to an Old Testament passage where King David celebrated before the Lord by leaping and dancing with all his might. Later criticized for this "undignified" praise, David believed his expressive offering pleased God.

A shout of frustration or despair might take on a totally different form. Shouters could uncork a flood of screams and, for some, even a physical outburst with arms flailing, tears streaming, and cries of anguish. Others took on a different demeanor, sometimes depending on the church denomination. As they felt their spirits lift, some danced or even sprinted laps around the church pews, transforming aisles into a makeshift track. And none of it felt new or unusual within the Black church. (Some predominantly white charismatic congregations practiced shouting, as well.)

"Shouting is rooted in African culture," says Jacquelyn Clemmons, an author and birth doula who has studied African dance and customs. Core movements in the church shout mimic motions popular in African dance styles. "Black people have always expressed a hop, a dance, a shout, a yell," she says. "That is who we are. That is what we do."

Clemmons recalls when her grandmother died. Rather than minimize her broken heart and express it as a quiet, polite whimper, she gave herself permission to weep and wail in what she calls a "soul cry." The release allowed her to let go of the pain and move toward healing. African Americans exercise this same kind of release weekly in Black churches. Sundays provide a time and place to weep, to let it all out in a safe space, in the company of others who understood.

"I feel like it's a tool that's been handed down to us from our ancestors to heal us," Clemmons says.

Shouting didn't happen every church service; nor did all believers catch the spirit, so to speak. But for those who did, they likely started off with a scream or yell, just as a piercing sermon concluded or when a particular song spoke to them. At Jerusalem Baptist in Fort Wayne, the minister of music during my childhood sang with a smooth, melodic voice. Mainly he played the organ for church hymns, the choir's songs, and as a backdrop throughout the service. But every now and then, just after the pastor preached, he would pause. Then he'd run his fingers lightly over those keys. Whenever this happened, I looked around to see if a well-known shouter sat close by, because the organist was about to sing, and we all knew what that meant: Somebody would shout. And I didn't want to be within arm's length of whoever that would be.

He started out softly with a modified version of an old Walter Hawkins tune, taking his time, strategically pausing and tapping those ivories.

What is this?

The sanctuary fell hush.

That I feel deep inside? What is this?

Whimpers broke the silence. Tears began to flow.

It keeps setting my soul afire. Whatever it i-i-isss, it won't let me hold my peace.

The first shouts rang out.

"Ooowww!"

"Je-suuus!"

Arms and legs flailed. The shouter was often a woman, and my mother and other ushers rushed to her side, encircling her to give room for the expression. For shouts of pain or frustration, ushers held her arms still to calm her. They placed scarves or their own suit jackets over her to shield stockinged calves and thighs from view. If she wore a hat or glasses, they removed them, set those aside. They waved paper fans to cool her down. Soon the arms stopped moving and screams subsided. Someone pulled out tissues to dry her tears. After the service, Mama came home worried about some woman who'd shouted that day.

From what I could tell, a frustrated shout typically signaled a low place in a woman's life. She was said to be "going through something," like the loss of a loved one, money problems, a child lost to the streets, a broken marriage, abuse, discrimination, and on and on. The sermon or the song lyrics or just her own thoughts somehow had pricked this area of pain, like a needle punctures a wound and causes pus to ooze in the healing process. A shouting woman released her distress through high screams and deep moans that escaped to the heavens, begging God for relief. A large painting of America's blond, straight-haired Jesus hung in the church, but I began to question whether that image authentically symbolized the God who responded to a Black woman's pain.

The shouting phenomenon, with all its tears and emotion, should not be confused with weakness, though. This I know because Big Mama used to shout, and people used a lot of adjectives and stories to describe her, but none included a weak will. For example, my mother tells a story of Big Mama's strength that begins with a dirty old man eyeing my youthful mother as she walked down the road. The man told someone what he wanted to do to my mother, if given the chance. Well, that person told Big Mama exactly what he said, and she didn't run to tell Granddaddy or any other man in the family. She would resolve the situation on her own. Big Mama simply went outside and picked up a field hoe. She gripped it behind her back and walked toward the man's house.

My mother saw her leaving. Confused, she asked, "Mama, what you got that hoe for?" Let's just say Big Mama returned home just as fine and calm as when she'd left. She put the hoe back in its place. She did not hurt the man, but from that day forward, he never touched or gave my mother a glance as she walked up and down the road.

No, Big Mama showed little sign of weakness or even being overly emotional, not typically. But at times she shouted, too. Life's struggles weighed her down, and she found release in the Lord's house. She cooked, oversaw much of the farm work, and made sure the kids picked cotton in the fields. She ruled as disciplinarian, even when it came to the boys. Well, *especially* when it came to the boys, which sometimes gave her reason enough to shout. Like the time when Willie James got much too big for his britches, as Big Mama would say. He smarted off at her about something and walked away, head held high and proud-like. He didn't get far before a slender stick of wood hit him on the head, knocking him sideways. Good thing no Department of Children and Families investigated in those backwoods, because a social worker would've charged Big Mama a hundred times over for throwing that stick straight at Willie James. (It wasn't the first time. She preferred a simple whupping, but if the kids ran to evade their punishment—or got sassy enough to just walk away like Willie James—she'd pick up some non-life-threatening item, aim, and throw. Like a skilled quarterback, she was known to hit her mark.)

Margaret "Big Mama" Page. *Page family photo*

Big Mama's disciplinary tactics were not uncommon in the Negro South and may seem comical to those familiar with the culture. But others, I know, find it cruel and barbaric. Some may think, "How could a mother do such a thing?" In the past, people assumed this style of corporal punishment must've originated in Africa, must be something engrained in Black culture or DNA. But none of that's true. Negroes simply did what they learned from slave masters. They grew up in slavery or were the descendants of slaves who'd observed and endured brutal beatings to force obedience. As parents, they then used those same methods on their children, having no other models to imitate. For Negroes, it seemed their parental duty to break the sass, the disobedience, and, in some ways, the independence out of children and make them yield without question to authority.

Studies show African Americans use corporal punishment significantly more than other racial groups in America. Scholars, psychologists, and other researchers link it to the lingering traumas of slavery, where discipline meant being whipped, beaten, killed, or separated from spouses, siblings, parents, or children. Slave mothers and fathers, then, adopted physical disciplinary tactics to mold their own children into tractable beings. The pressure had to be overwhelming since rebellion or a strong will could lead to death or being sold off and never seen again. Then, after slavery, the culture of demeaning Blacks and the violence against them continued, at the hands of torturous white supremacists and Jim Crow laws, and so did Blacks' fears. At least that's how some experts explain it. Still, corporal punishment, in its varying forms, is not exclusive to Black Americans. Other cultures engage in the practice, and many who believe in spankings or other physical discipline, at least to some degree, say it has divine roots. They quote a biblical proverb to prove it: "Spare the rod, spoil the child."

Just one generation removed from the Emancipation Proclamation, Big Mama grew up with the same corporal punishment that her parents had experienced from their parents on their masters' plantations. When it came to her own kids, she did not spare the rod, like those before her. No one doubted her love for the family. She had to keep it all together, had to keep those kids in line—the only way she knew how. And, sometimes, it hurt her, too. I believe this because after she taught Willie James a lesson with that wooden stick, Big Mama went to church later that day. During service, the tears flowed first, then came the scream, and Big Mama shouted, crying out to God. Exactly what she cried out for, no one today knows. But my uncle Howard, a young adult at the time, witnessed it all, from the backtalk to the wood slap to the shout. He couldn't help but laugh and make a joke out of what seemed like a paradox. "Well, you beat Willie James," he'd say, "then you go to church and shout your shoes off!"

Personally, I never shouted. As the years wear on and my mother's generation grows older, the practice seems to be fading from many Black churches. These days, I've seen it less frequently and, even then, in toned-down fashion. Still, I understand those shouts so much better than I did as a child scooting away to avoid chaos. I understand partly because I've felt burdened by the stresses of living as a Black woman in America, where I am the so-called "double minority," seen by some as inferior twice over because of my skin color and gender. The strains it takes to prove myself, my skills, my worth within a dominant white society sometimes feel like too much. The subtle but clear jabs of discrimination against people of color and women, the hurtful rhetoric becoming more acceptable in our nation, can be deflating. On top of that come life's routine responsibilities and worries. There are times when it all makes me want to scream, too, to shout for help from God.

I'm not alone. Black women suffer from stress more than other groups. Indeed, some experts say it's killing us. We have lower life expectancy and higher rates of stroke and heart disease than white women. Life stresses us all, but experts have called out the disproportionate levels of stress that Blacks experience, especially Black women. They link stress among African Americans to unequal rates of high blood pressure and even diabetes. Dealing with the anxiety of discrimination, the feelings of being perceived as less than, and all those seemingly slight microaggressions piling up inside, affecting our minds, actions, and our physical bodies—taking everything into account, I see why my sisters of old shouted, especially those in the charismatic-style churches that embraced it. I see why they carried those shouts from the South to the Midwest.

Like me, Clemmons has noticed the decrease in shouting since her childhood days. We theorized that the blueprint for some Black churches has changed, including a shorter service, among other things that leave little room for shouts and dancing in the aisles. Some see the practice as outdated. Clemmons, on the other hand, says the shift is not ideal.

"Think about the pain, the trauma in the church pews that those people were experiencing," she said. "I don't think it's a good thing that we don't have a space to do that."

While shouting followed the migrants north, some traditions stayed in the South. They didn't bring the mourning bench, for instance. My mother mentioned it only briefly in my childhood, so salvation came much easier for us. One day in youth choir practice, the instructor asked who had not been baptized. I raised my hand. She asked if we believed Jesus died for our sins, and I said yes. I went home and told Mama, and she believed I had accepted Jesus. Soon, I stood in the church basement, surrounded by deacons singing in baritone, "Going to the water. Going to the water." Somebody led a line of us kids to the baptismal pool. I stood barefoot, wearing a swim cap and a white tunic made from a sheet, at age nine. I closed my eyes. One of the ministers dunked me, pressing me into the cool water, then lifting me up for my symbolic rebirth in Christ.

Years later, as a young adult with deeper understanding, I elected to be baptized again, recommitting my life to the faith. In adulthood, I paid more attention to my mother's stories about the bench, about getting religion. By then, I knew for myself that times would come when faith proved my greatest weapon and most resistant shield. I understood the importance of spirituality in our family from Granddaddy's day till now. I could feel the meaning in those old church lyrics.

Have you got good religion?
Certainly, Lord. Certainly, certainly, certainly, Lord.

CHAPTER SEVEN

POLICING MOONSHINE AND MURDER

GRANDDADDY'S ACCIDENT fed conversation around Browns and Uniontown for some time, considering the newspaper article in the *Selma Times-Journal*, Granddaddy's position as a local pastor, and the fact that a man in uniform hit him. People talked about it, analyzed the consequences on wooden porch swings, in the church yard after service, at the Sundown Ranch. They waited to see if Talladega County would pay up for totaling Granddaddy's car and for his injured arm. After all, even the white men with the state highway patrol faulted Deputy Lee, and he was on duty at the time.

Amid all the talking, life churned on for Granddaddy and Big Mama, but with more problems than before. He couldn't work, so no pay came from Radford & Son. With eight children still depending on him at home, he ran out of options quick. The family shopped quite a bit at a store nearby, buying flour, cornmeal, and other staples they couldn't grow for themselves. A friend at the store saw how Granddaddy and Big Mama struggled to pay for what they needed. He had an idea to ease the burden, Willie James says. They could use that program President Franklin D. Roosevelt put in place almost twenty years earlier. The Social Security Act offered help to families that lost a breadwinner, which meant a working man in those days since women, like Big Mama, rarely worked outside of their homes. People later called aspects of the program welfare. Granddaddy got the paperwork and applied. Soon food stamps helped fill the gaps at home. It didn't amount to much, though, and the situation needled some around town, seeing that neither the deputy nor Talladega County paid Granddaddy what rightfully belonged to him.

If the skin colors were reversed, if Granddaddy had crashed into a white man, he would have paid him. That much we know for sure because it actually happened. Willie James says Granddaddy was driving with a relative in the car when they came to a bridge. The driver in front of him stopped, and, before anybody knew better, Granddaddy's Chevy rear-ended the man. This happened some time before they got him, my uncle said.

The other driver, a local cow farmer, jumped out of his car, cussing and carrying on, ready to beat Granddaddy down. He might have tried, except another witness calmed him. No need to harm Preacher Page over a fender bender. Granddaddy, meanwhile, promised to make good on the damages. The repair bill turned out to be somewhere around $160, Willie James says. That amounted to a good deal of money, more than some of the paychecks Granddaddy earned for working weeks on a well-drilling project. Thankfully, Granddaddy's Prince Hall fraternity brothers pitched in to pay it. They knew what angry white men did to Negroes in the South for a lot less than a bruised bumper or taillight. That man must've been shocked—and maybe a little bitter, too—when Granddaddy came up with the money and delivered it to him, after all. If everything happened the way Willie James remembers it, I'm sure Granddaddy reflected on that accident and his own accountability when calculating his next move toward justice.

Consequences and accountability tended to shift when a Negro sat in the victim's seat. A hundred miles away from Browns, the accident between Granddaddy and Deputy Lee reached another broad audience. In Talladega County, where the deputy lived, word spread that Brantley Lee, one of their chief law enforcement officers, had crashed into a Negro. Talladega was much bigger than Dallas or Perry Counties, where Granddaddy lived. Back in the 1950s, Talladega County boasted nearly 64,000 people in its cities and unincorporated areas. Talladega City to the north and Sylacauga and Childersburg to the south were the county's largest cities. Perry, on the other hand, had shrunk to about 20,000 people, losing more than 20 percent of its population since 1930. Dallas County, which Perry straddled and where Browns technically existed, had about 56,000. Yet Browns, the little area where Granddaddy and Big Mama's house sat, counted only 556 people in 1950, down from nearly 1,300 twenty years earlier.

Curiously, some newspapers in Talladega never mentioned Granddaddy or even acknowledged the second car involved. The articles make vague references to Lee being in an "accident" and name the people in his car. A story headlined "Talladega County Deputy; Two Others Injured in Wreck Near Selma Sunday" mentioned that Lee and his brother-in-law "received minor injuries," while his brother suffered a broken leg and fractured ribs and was hospitalized. The "Negro patient being taken by county officers to the mental hospital in Mount

Vernon was the only one of four car occupants to escape injury in a weekend accident," the report reads. (The accident actually took place on a weekday, Thursday.) The *Talladega News* reported that Lee had suffered cuts and bruises in an accident that wrecked his cruiser and that he had returned to work. That paper named Lee's passengers but mentioned nothing about a second car or Granddaddy.

Maybe reporters intended to be vague. Maybe they recorded limited information because that's what the sheriff's office gave them. Still, residents learned the details, because officials discussed the case in public meetings, causing the crash to stir up talk throughout Talladega just as it did in Browns and Uniontown. That much would have been a given with Lee's status in the community. He and just three or so other deputies, plus the sheriff, made up the countywide sheriff's department back then.

Deputy Lee and a partner patrolled the southern end of the county, an on-call job that he reported to whenever duty called. When it didn't, he busied himself in the textile industry, working for a time at the Danville Knitting Mill. His wife worked there for a time, too, and a housekeeper lived with them, perhaps taking care of their young daughter. People knew Lee likewise from his work with local elections over the years, serving as returning officer and election manager for local districts.

But being a man of the law seemed to be his most prestigious job, at least for a while. Sheriff Earl Howell shared the ups and downs of working as a Talladega deputy with a local reporter in 1953. Howell sketched what it looked like to work on his force, including the round-the-clock schedule and the sense of service they felt when helping others.

"So, why is anyone a policeman?" the reporter asked.

"I don't know," Sheriff Howell said. "After a fellow gets started, he doesn't mind too bad. He helps folks, settles their troubles. That makes him feel good."

The reporter went on to write about the potential for harm. "With every call they answer county officers face potential danger," the article reads. "And the major danger doesn't always come from the greatest offenders, although generally the greater the offense the greater safety precautions officers take. But minor cases of vagrancy and non-support are bundled [sic] with care."

The sheriff explained, "A fellow with family trouble, especially if he's drinking, might give trouble."

For the most part, law enforcement in Talladega didn't rankle the deputies much. A lot of their work amounted to giving information to the public when it came to law enforcement and courts. "There are no real outlaws in this county," the sheriff said. "Those we arrest are not usually real criminals." Generally speaking, he said, moonshiners were the most peaceful class of all offenders. "They'll run," Sheriff Howell said, "but they don't shoot."

Deputies also settled domestic disputes, including husbands and wives who "wanted their spouses arrested for stepping out." In those cases, deputies explained, "it isn't against the law for people to go together," the sheriff said. In the end, deputies encountered headaches but not boredom. According to the article: "They seldom get a full night's sleep, either."

The sheriff's descriptions aside, Talladega and its law enforcement should not be likened to TV's lowkey fictional town of Mayberry. Moonshining kept deputies on their toes, including some big busts, as well as some gruesome discoveries, assaults, and murder. The government repealed prohibition laws nationally in 1933, but some Alabama communities opted to stay dry within their borders for decades afterward. Some counties in the state technically still upheld prohibition laws well into the twenty-first century, although cities within those counties may have legalized alcohol within city limits. One night in 1950, a team including a state investigator, the sheriff, Lee, and other deputies descended on a legion club in Childersburg. The bust confiscated twenty cases of bear, two slot machines, and a pint of whiskey.

Lee's name can be linked to a flurry of other intriguing cases during the time. It was Lee who appeared on the scene of a dead newborn baby. Animals had sniffed out the corpse and scratched the baby from a shallow grave. Children passing by made the gruesome discovery and reported it. Doctors could not identify the body or the cause of death, declaring only that the baby was likely white.

Lee also got the tip on the whereabouts of a father whose son died of pneumonia and malnutrition. Officers searched for the man for two weeks before someone whispered in Lee's ear, and authorities found the man in Shelby County.

And Lee helped investigate the killing of a raging drunk Negro who wielded an ax and threatened to kill his stepson. The stepson got the better of him, killing him with a claw hammer instead. He then ran to a white neighbor's house, told what he'd done, and used the neighbor's phone to call authorities to pick him up.

The Talladega sheriff's department, itself, held no immunity to disorder and violence. In 1948, for instance, Lee's two main jobs collided when he investigated a mysterious murder and shooting that left the Danville mill offices in "bloody shambles" and a fellow deputy deceased. The mill employed about two hundred people at the time, and the company clerk found two victims when he got to work that morning. Dan Pierce was dead; another man, critically injured. Like Lee, Pierce worked at the mill and doubled as a sheriff's deputy. That morning, a coworker who first saw the horrific scene scurried to find Lee, who launched an investigation into the crime.

And just months after Sheriff Howell's mild newspaper interview in 1953 about deputies' routine workday, Howell asked Lee's partner, Deputy John Jones, to surrender his badge for undisclosed reasons. Howell said only that he asked for the resignation "in order to get the best possible for the county." Then, a year later, in October 1954, Howell held a 41 Derringer to his own right temple and pulled the trigger. He left no suicide note. He'd recently lost a bid for reelection and had a "serious operation" of some sort. His wife served out the few months remaining in his term.

By the time of Howell's death, Lee had been deemed chief deputy, working closely with Howell and, later, his wife. It seemed a busy time for the husband and father. On Tuesday, July 12, with Howell still alive and in charge, Chief Deputy Lee helped investigate the murder of a thirty-six-year-old maid and member of a prominent Negro family in Sylacauga. The woman and her husband were saving to buy a home, and people knew she carried a large sum of money "on her person." Her husband reported her missing, and a taxi driver happened upon her strangled body the next day. Her savings, $700, was missing. Lee and other officials worked potential leads through the night, then traveled that Wednesday about 150 miles to Americus, Georgia, to interview a potential suspect. Besides Lee, the solicitor, another deputy, and a state toxicologist made the trip. They didn't get enough for an arrest, and they all returned to Alabama late Wednesday. The case held the county's interest, of course, especially with the murderer still at-large. Still, Lee had other duties to tend to, as well. The very next day, Thursday, July 15, 1954, he would head out on another work trip—this time a journey to transport a Negro to the Mount Vernon Hospital for the Colored Insane.

The asylum, itself, is a story, a symbol of inequity and injustice for people of color in Alabama. The site originally operated as one of the nation's first military arsenals, beginning in the early 1800s. During the Civil War, Confederates controlled the site, although it reverted to the US military again postwar. At one point, the Mount Vernon facility housed four hundred Chiricahua Apache Native Americans as prisoners of war—although none were actually charged with crimes.

By 1900, some medical professionals noticed an increase in the reported number of mentally ill Negroes after the Reconstruction era. (Not surprising, considering the trauma that must have followed the end of slavery and America's failure to help former slaves establish themselves and reap the full benefits of American citizenship.) This increase led to overcrowding at the Alabama State Hospital for the Insane in Tuscaloosa, and the state set aside money to renovate and repurpose the Mount Vernon arsenal.

Segregation set the standard for businesses, restrooms, and schools, so Alabama leaders felt it should expand to the mentally ill, too. The Mount Vernon asylum materialized at the turn of the twentieth century, separating Negroes from their white counterparts at the hospital in Tuscaloosa. The Mount Vernon complex, now abandoned and known as the old Searcy Hospital, is listed on the National Register of Historic Places. It had existed for decades simply to avoid mingling white mental illness with Black mental illness. For this reason, Deputy Lee couldn't take the reportedly insane thirty-nine-year-old Lewis Hamilton to Tuscaloosa, just 100 miles away. Segregation added 150 more miles to his trek, for a 250-mile day trip to Mount Vernon.

His brother, Samuel "S. S." Lee, and brother-in-law would help him manage the journey. Lee even "deputized" the civilian Samuel before the trip, granting him some of a law officer's powers, such as making an arrest. (It's unclear whether the brother-in-law got the same treatment.) The three relatives and Hamilton took a straightforward route at the time, hitting State Road 5 and taking it south. They likely passed Heiberger and Marion, approaching the Uniontown area intersecting with Highway 80, a major east-west thoroughfare.

Who knows what they talked about over the two and a half or three hours up to that point? Perhaps Deputy Lee updated them on twists in the Negro maid's murder. Or maybe he talked about tracking down a drunk man sipping moonshine or a fight between a husband and wife. Or he might have set aside work altogether for family business with his relatives. Whatever the case, he got distracted somehow, just as State Road 5 met Highway 80. His cruiser should have stopped and let cars on the highway pass him by. If he had, Granddaddy's Chevy would've disappeared from view, and the deputy's car would've crossed the highway, continuing on 5 toward Mount Vernon.

Instead, the evidence pointed to a typical T-bone accident. Highway patrol officers faulted Lee for reckless driving and failure to stop at a stop sign. A cut-and-dried case if there ever was one. When the Dallas County Circuit Court in Selma opened months later for its December term, the docket listed Brantley

Lee's name. Officials dismissed the reckless driving charge, but Lee paid a fine of "$50 and costs for failing to stop at a stop sign." The *Selma Times-Journal* listed that fine among a series of routine court actions in December 1954. It may have easily gone unnoticed in Browns, and in Talladega, too, for that matter. But Talladega officials certainly knew that Lee accepted his negligence and paid the fine. They reached out to Granddaddy more than once and heard his side of what happened. Still, nothing ever came of it. The payout he hoped for did not materialize. No check arrived, not from Talladega County and not from Deputy Lee, as if they all hoped in time that he would just go away.

CHAPTER EIGHT

—∿∿—

A COUNTRY LAWYER

SURGEONS AT VAUGHAN MEMORIAL operated on Granddaddy's right arm in September, so he had recovered as best he could by the time Deputy Lee paid that $50 fine for failing to stop. They couldn't restore his arm, and the family's hope did not lead to healing, not this time. That limb would forever hang limp at Granddaddy's side, a thing for strangers to stare at, for grandchildren to wonder about in the years to come. With the hospital stays, the surgery, and all that came with it, Granddaddy racked up $3,486 in medical costs, the equivalent of about $36,000 today.

Around Browns, folks talked about the potential of Preacher Page filing a lawsuit. Not only had the bills kept coming, but now they knew he couldn't go back to drilling wells. Men uptown and at the Sundown Ranch suggested lawyers they'd heard of in the area. Family members, on the other hand, wanted him to find an attorney in Birmingham, maybe even a Negro, like the ones who worked for the NAACP. A couple of Granddaddy's brothers had moved to Birmingham, working in steel factories there. They figured big-city attorneys, even the white ones, had a more progressive mindset and might try harder to help a Black man than a country lawyer would.

People had to know that a lawsuit would stir up a world of trouble. Suing a white sheriff's deputy took a heap of gumption or, more than likely, a heap of faith. After all, Granddaddy served a God who called him and his children one by one to get religion. This was the God they'd fasted for, to whom they cried and shouted for mercy. He was the same God who gave David a slingshot and five smooth stones, then sent him to battle a nine-foot-tall giant named Goliath. By the grace of God, the unworthy shepherd boy boldly stated his case in Goliath's face, slung one stone, and won the fight. That God, Granddaddy believed, could lead a Negro sharecropper and well driller to prevail against a white man with a badge in Jim Crow Alabama.

On the other hand, I can fathom how the lawsuit didn't seem that far-fetched, even for the rural South at the time. The car accident occurred two months after the US Supreme Court issued its landmark decision in Brown v. Board of Education, which desegregated public schools—at least on paper. The high court's ruling sparked some optimism among Negroes about change. Never mind that Granddaddy only had a third-grade education before he left the classroom for the cotton field. He still read a lot, to the point where one of his brothers nicknamed him "Book," so he had likely either read about the court case or heard about it uptown, on the radio, or at the Sundown Ranch. Whites in the South feared what blacks at the time hoped—that a ruling denouncing the old "separate but equal" lie in education just might filter into other parts of the law. Indeed, it might give Blacks the vision to fight for true equality.

Considering the God of justice and a seeming political shift, victory appeared probable, if not inevitable. No need to insist on a big-city lawyer, Granddaddy figured. That would buck his style anyway. He didn't like traveling far off the rural path. From Granddaddy's view, nothing compared to country living, where people sat on porches in rocking chairs and waved at folks passing by. Where you could look for miles and see nothing but the land God saw fit to create. Where a man took his time, strolled with his hands in his pockets and a whistle between his lips. Nothing Granddaddy heard on the radio about city folk or northerners impressed him enough to want it for himself. Not working on a factory assembly line, not eating hamburgers from strangers in fast-food restaurants, not living close enough to hear the family next door or wearing fancy clothes from big stores.

Few people remember Granddaddy going much of anywhere outside the state of Alabama, so that time he came to Fort Wayne sticks out. It happened years after the accident, in the late 1960s, when one of his brothers tricked him. He told Granddaddy they were going for a ride. Once inside the car, they just kept driving and driving. Somewhere along the way, Granddaddy realized they'd left Alabama, but he couldn't do a thing about it. LeRoy Page drove Granddaddy all the way to Fort Wayne and my parents' house. Unimpressed with all the streets and concrete sidewalks, the houses side by side, Granddaddy declared, "I'll walk home." But, of course, his legs couldn't carry him seven hundred miles. He stayed for about a week before LeRoy drove him back down south. The Great Migration of Blacks had been transpiring for decades at this point, but Granddaddy didn't see much sense in it all. Mind you, this trip occurred years after they got him, and Granddaddy still lacked any desire to leave the South. Many people thought Negroes fared better in the city, better than in the backwoods South where Granddaddy lived. But like most things, *better* is a matter of perspective.

All that said, Granddaddy settled on a country lawyer, not far from Browns. He wanted to keep up with the case's progress, according to Willie James. That meant finding someone close, never mind a liberal from Birmingham. Not many, if any, Negro lawyers existed around those parts, and as far as Grand-daddy could tell, a white man in the country couldn't be too much different than a white man in the city. The decision didn't sit well with some, but Grand-daddy's relationship with Mr. Radford gave him a trust for white folks that escaped others in his day.

Neighbors' reservations about the way Granddaddy handled the case aside, something else, something more basic, didn't sit well with me either, not ini-tially anyway. The Granddaddy I came to know had a genteel way about him that didn't quite fit with a take-it-to-court mentality. He didn't threaten people or put his foot down much; he didn't even spank his children. In fact, he seemed to brush off snickers from progressive Negroes of the day who looked down on his large family and country life. Then came that accident, and that mild manner didn't work for him. Hospital bills kept coming, and the family needed money to survive. And now I could see why even a man like him went further than he normally would to gain justice. I saw how desperation lured the fight out of a man like nothing else. I can't help but imagine him thinking about Dave strutting around with boldness on his chest. That didn't suit Granddaddy at all, but he wanted a little piece of the respect that Dave held tight, too. He wanted respect outside of the church walls, I suppose, respect in his manhood and his right to make a living. So he got a lawyer—nobody famous but someone with a big enough name around Browns and Uniontown. About twenty miles north, in Marion, Granddaddy talked to a man by the name of Sheldon Fitts Sr.

Like Granddaddy, Fitts grew up in Alabama, born in nearby Chilton County in 1899. He'd traveled a much different path than Granddaddy, though, a path dotted with sports and letterman pins, travel, and mentions in the *Selma Times-Journal* society pages. White people in the area knew Fitts and knew him well. Fitts's father, the sheriff of Chilton County, died when Fitts was young. Fitts and his mother later moved to the Uniontown area and lived with his stepfather. He became a star baseball player for a local team there. Later, as a student at Georgia Military College and the University of Georgia, he lettered in football and baseball. He graduated from the Chicago-Kent School of Law, then worked as a claims investigator and practicing attorney in Chicago, New York City, and

Canada. By the time Granddaddy met him, he lived in the city of Marion, in Perry County, where he'd represented clients for more than a decade.

News articles featured him and his wife, Frances, a Chicago native. Even minor mentions with the Fitts name proved of interest to the area's elite. "Sheldon Fitts . . . is visiting his parents, Mr. and Mrs. T.I. Ward at Hamburg." "Miss Ruth Barlow, who is attending the Chicago Fair, is the guest of Mrs. Sheldon Fitts, of Chicago." "More than 100 entries are expected for the Marion Horse Show. . . . Sheldon Fitts will announce the show." "Mr. and Mrs. Harvey Vernon Link, of Chattanooga, announce the engagement of their daughter, Beverly Ann, to Sheldon Fitts, Jr., son of Mr. and Mrs. Sheldon Fitts, of Marion."

In 1950, Fitts gained greater recognition when he campaigned to become the new circuit solicitor of Alabama's fourth judicial circuit. He bought newspaper ads and made his voice heard in the months leading up to the vote. On election day in May, Fitts garnered nearly three times as many votes as his opponent did in Perry County, a display of his notoriety in his hometown. He lost the election, though. The incumbent, James Hare, carried the other four counties in the circuit.

Fitts's political aspirations faded from public view, and he continued practicing law and living on his dairy farm. It's not clear exactly when Granddaddy secured Fitts's representation. Months passed without any known documented action, even after Lee paid his court fine. One might think Talladega officials would have finalized a settlement with Granddaddy after Lee paid the fine, but they didn't. Some Page family members speculated about Fitts's commitment to help a Negro, but Granddaddy stayed with him. And the family's faith got a boost on July 11, 1955, just four days before the accident's one-year anniversary. Fitts and another attorney, Judson C. Locke, did indeed file a case in the circuit court of Dallas County, Alabama: *Israel Page vs. Brantley Lee.*

The other lawyer was also a state legislator, so people knew the name Judson Locke all over Alabama—white people that is. Many Negroes didn't bother with voting, especially in rural areas. Whites imposed extra rules to stop Negroes from casting ballots, so some didn't even try. Besides, voting for circuit solicitors and state legislators had little meaning, since officials rarely fought for Negroes' rights. They didn't know Judson Locke or Sheldon Fitts from Yul Brynner. (It's unclear whether Locke played a significant role in the case or acted as a consultant when needed. My uncles only remember Fitts.)

Fifty years later, when that clerk in Selma found my grandfather's lawsuit in the basement of the Dallas County Courthouse, I felt as if it had waited for me, waited to be unearthed and brought back to life. The suit asked for $8,500 in damages, the equivalent of about $80,000 today. It justified the claim in a winding run-on sentence that apparently took on Fitts's style of writing lawsuits.

> The defendant did negligently and carelessly run his automobile into the plaintiff's automobile, completely demolishing and damaging plaintiff's automobile, and the plaintiff was permanently and severely injured and was so injured that as a proximate consequence thereof his right arm was broken, the right ulna and right radial nerve in his right arm are a complete loss; and the plaintiff received a crushing blow to his head and was knocked and rendered unconscious, shocked, bruised, strained and sprained in each and every part of his body and plaintiff was rendered for a long time unable to work and earn money and is at the time of the filing of this complaint unable to perform his usual type of work and earn money; and plaintiff was put to great trouble, inconvenience and expense, in that, he was confined to the hospital, expended large sums of money for medical attention, doctor's bills, in his efforts to heal and cure his said wounds and injuries; plaintiff further avers the damage to his automobile and the injuries to his person complained of are the proximate result of the negligence of the defendant for all of which the plaintiff claims damages as aforesaid.

The response from Lee and his attorney, Wesley R. Smith, made it clear they had no plans of paying up. They outlined eleven points for rebuttal. The suit was vague and lacked proof, they said. It wasn't worded properly. Perhaps the craziest rebuttal point was this: "For aught that appears, Plaintiff had no right to be where he was at the time and place of said accident." In other words, Granddaddy shouldn't have been driving on that highway in the first place. The argument is baffling and may point to the historical racism of the time. It's as if Lee and his lawyer thought to themselves, *Well, wait a minute—what was that Negro doing driving around anyway? Who does he think he is—an American citizen or something?*

They also made these claims:

"No facts are alleged to show that Plaintiff sustained any damage or injury as the proximate result of any negligence or breach of duty on the part of the defendant."

"It is not alleged with sufficient certainty where said accident occurred."

"The alleged negligence of the Defendant is not set forth with sufficient certainty."

Obviously, the legal strategy aimed to cast doubt that the accident caused any harm or that it even occurred in the first place. Now here's where things get even more perplexing. Lee and his attorney, Smith, filed this response on

Tuesday, August 2, 1955—again calling into question Lee's negligence, where the accident occurred, and whether Granddaddy sustained any damages or injury. Yet, less than a week later, on Monday, August 8, Lee took a totally different stance at the county commission meeting in Talladega, a hundred miles from where he filed this response to Granddaddy's claim.

By this time, some interesting developments had taken place. For one, Lee no longer worked for the sheriff's office. After Sheriff Howell's suicide, incoming sheriff John Robinson brought in a team of new deputies as his term began in January. Lee was not among them. Second, Lee's brother, Samuel S. Lee— the one who got a broken leg and fractured ribs—decided he wanted damages from the accident, too, and Brantley Lee didn't object. In fact, he supported his brother's claim to get paid. The Lee brothers felt the county should pay up, since Lee ran the stop sign while officially on the job and his brother had been deputized. During the county commission meeting on August 8, former deputy Brantley Lee, whose driving had caused it all, stood by Sam's side. Unlike the rebuttal in court documents filed in Granddaddy's case, here no one questioned that Lee had driven the car or where the accident had happened. A reporter who covered the commission meeting referred to Brantley Lee by his nickname, "Monk Lee." The article, in the *Talladega Daily Home and Our Mountain Home* newspaper archives, reads: "The accident occurred at the intersection of Highways 80 and 5 as Monk Lee and his brother were returning 'a crazy Negro' to Mount Vernon, asylum for Negroes, Lee told the commissioners. He admitted that he did not stop for the sign, saying he slowed down and then drove on when he did not see anything coming."

During this commission meeting, no one disputed that Granddaddy deserved to be compensated, at least to some degree. The Lee brothers had a spokesman, Representative L. N. Payne, who proposed a settlement that included Granddaddy, as well as Sam Lee. "Payne asked that the commissioners award Sam Lee $750 'or as much as you will' and award a Negro, Israel Page, $750 for injuries received when the county car driven by Monk Lee allegedly ran a stop sign and collided with the Negro's car at Marion Junction last year," the article states.

Brantley Lee probably hoped the county would pay off Granddaddy, instead of him having to do so himself, since Granddaddy's lawsuit named him alone as defendant. At one point, the commissioners debated whether they could offer Granddaddy $500 to settle his claim, and Payne said he'd ask him. Whether Granddaddy would have accepted $500 or $750 when his actual hospital bills totaled more than $3,000 sounds like a stretch, but even that was more than what the county could give him anyway, at least without permission from the state. Granddaddy's and Sam Lee's injuries exceeded the amount Talladega County could authorize without state approval, according to Probate Judge D. Hardy Riddle, who argued against settlements.

During that time, it seems, the county reserved $300 a year to settle minor disputes. To get around the cap, officials had to get state legislators to pass a special bill. A minority of commissioners initially voted to introduce such a bill in the state legislature. They wanted to ask for $750 each for Granddaddy and Sam Lee, but the majority voted them down. Over the next eighteen months, Sam Lee would go back and forth with the county, seeking damages that ranged from $750 to $2,000. Finally, in February 1957, two and a half years after the accident, commissioners agreed to ask the state legislature to give Sam Lee $1,000 in damages. Legislators complied, ending the dispute once and for all.

Granddaddy's name gradually faded from these negotiations. Perhaps he and Fitts refused to take the meager amount the commissioners offered since his injuries were much more extensive and permanent than Sam Lee's, and he could no longer work to support his family. I found no indication that the commissioners also sought legislative approval to give Granddaddy a higher settlement. We do know that his case lingered in the courthouse, and nothing about it moved quickly. Indeed, the court folder showed no official paperwork filed for two and a half years, from fall 1955 until 1958. The case file may be incomplete, lacking some court filings. Or maybe Fitts negotiated verbally with Talladega County during that time. Maybe he waited to see if the commissioners would ask the state to grant Granddaddy a larger settlement. Another possibility: Fitts and Locke were busy with other cases between Negroes and whites, of which there were plenty in the 1950s and beyond. Eventually, I found evidence that the latter might be true. In the middle of Granddaddy's case, his attorneys sank knee-deep in another case that highlighted America's racially lopsided court system and unearthed Fitts's peculiar views of white privilege and justice for all.

CHAPTER NINE

—꽈—

GOOD TIMES MEETS *THE BRADY BUNCH*

GRANDDADDY'S STORY gave me a richer perspective of white privilege, how it had played out in his life and mine, too. I wondered when he understood his lesser status, compared to the white boys who lived uptown, that is. Did the revelation come early on when family warned him against looking at a white woman or eyeballing white men during trips into town? Or did the truth of his status come more organically, a feeling that crept into his spirit simply by way of existing in an America so segregated by skin color?

For me, the reckoning came gradually. As a little girl, I used to sit cross-legged on the carpet in front of our wood-framed TV, soaking in the scenes of *The Brady Bunch* and *Happy Days*. My mind automatically contrasted the white characters' childhood squabbles and hijinks to the more serious and relatable plots of *Good Times* and *What's Happening*, sitcoms featuring Black families. The Black characters often struggled to overcome money problems, while holding onto a sense of family, of togetherness, much like we did in our home.

The differences fueled curiosity about my white classmates at school, and I became intentional about interacting with them. In addition to Black friends who rode the bus with me, I hung out with the white kids, too. They interested me. They didn't watch *Good Times* or *Fat Albert*—this I knew because they seemed clueless of the cultural divides and traditions separating us. They assumed, for instance, that all people washed their hair in the shower daily, despite our differing hair textures. I imagine Granddaddy held a measure of curiosity about the whites he encountered, too, taking in their ways of life and customs, comparing them with his own, then deciding to eat his eggs runny rather than scrambled hard.

The Tubbs family, including mother Julia, son Arbra, Deborah, and youngest daughter, Sharon (John Tubbs not pictured). *Tubbs family photo*

For me the worlds collided daily. When I left home and entered the halls of my integrated elementary school, I sat between two white students, since Blacks were so sparse. Sometimes we played together at recess. We ate lunch side by side in the cafeteria, typically whatever meal the ladies with hairnets handed out. One girl always brought her lunch, because she had diabetes. The rest of us looked forward to the best meal of the week—the one with square slices of pizza in tin containers.

After school, I rode the bus home and unlocked the door to an empty house. Soon my brother and sister arrived from middle or high school. Mama had made breakfast and saw us off to school but left for work before we got home. She put dinner on the stove, so we warmed it up, prepared our plates, and ate at different times, often while watching TV. If we didn't like what she cooked (squash or liver and rice were a no for me), we made a sandwich, which meant two slices of bread with bologna or maybe peanut butter and jelly or tuna salad. When my father got home from a long day at the factory, he ate and took a nap. If I asked later that night, he'd let me sit on his lap while he read one of my book club books from school. My brother, sister, and I took turns washing dishes. Mama got home just before midnight. Sometimes on Fridays, she wouldn't cook at all, so we called my father at work and convinced him to pick up a pizza.

I felt content, but the TV shows drove me to compare my life with the images of white childhood. Did their lives mirror *The Brady Bunch* and the old ABC Afterschool Specials series with moral themes? I inserted my peers into TV scenes, seeing them leaving school, merrily walking home, or riding bikes rather than getting off the yellow bus, like me. I saw them entering the front door and, for some reason, announcing their presence with a high-pitched, "Hi, Mom!" or a singsong "Mo-*om*! I'm ho-*ome*!" Then, of course, they'd gather around a lengthy maple dinner table, passing matching dishes filled with mashed potatoes, gravy, and semibloody pot roast, chatting and grinning with joy.

Friendships with white girls intrigued me. I remember one girl, Michelle, told me a story offhandedly. Something had happened the day before with another student or teacher at school—I can't recall fully. The details she relayed afterward stuck with me. When Michelle got home, her stay-at-home mom sensed something wrong, Michelle said, but she just wanted to be alone. A bit later, when her father got home from the office, they all ate dinner together, before she again retreated to her room. Her father noticed something was wrong and went to her room, sat with her, and talked. I envisioned him sitting on the edge of her bed, gingerly asking questions and listening as she revealed the details of her elementary school saga. He encouraged her, Michelle said, and made her feel better.

She was sincere and heartfelt, but the whole thing rang overly dramatic to me at the time, something reserved for white households, a scene scripted from the make-believe drama of Mike and Carol Brady. I acted as a childhood journalist even then, asking questions to draw out the minutiae of this episode brought to life. The stay-at-home mom. The family meal around a dining room table. The father arriving home from the office, then reserving time to discuss the major family problem of the day—not a bill that must get paid, a car in need of repairs, or the reasons behind a shout of anguish at church but a childhood spat from the halls of an elementary school. White kids, I learned, saw life and importance from a different angle. Many of them didn't think about the issues my siblings and I did.

The contrast glared more starkly during a class field trip to the zoo. We all had to bring a lunch from home, and I felt some anxiety about this. By now I knew our home life, including our food, differed from that of my white class-mates. The school lunches put us all on an equal playing field, but now I wasn't sure how to bridge the gap. The night before, I neatly spread mayonnaise on two slices of bread, placed a piece of bologna between, and cut the sandwich in half diagonally to make it look neat. I debated using foil or wax paper to wrap it, eventually deciding on a sheet of stiff wax paper, just like my father used when he took his lunch to the factory. I put it inside a tin lunch box from the clearance bin at Walgreens, along with a bag of potato chips and a Faygo pop. I wanted everything to look just right.

The teacher had split the students into pairs, and I would be partnered with another white friend, Stephanie, and her mom, who came along to chaperone. (My mother couldn't come, of course, because she had to work.) Off we went that day, leaving from the school on a yellow bus and arriving shortly at the local zoo, a place I had never been. I'm sure it was an experience to be trea-sured, although I don't recall delighting in the adventure of seeing animals up close. I don't remember talking to caged lions or monkeys or birds or be-ing interested in what they ate. I may have felt that way in the moment, but what lingers in my mind about my first trip to the zoo is something altogether different: lunch.

Another of Stephanie's friends, Lisa, and Lisa's mom joined us at our picnic table in the pavilion. When I got my lunch box, I noticed that Stephanie's and Lisa's mothers didn't have similar tin carriers. They pulled out mini coolers, instead, their food securely packaged in the temperature-controlled containers. Clear plastic wrap sealed their sandwiches nicely, just like in the stores. And, oh, what sandwiches they were! Theirs were the sandwiches of Afterschool Specials, much thicker than my single-bologna-slice creation. Each had several pieces of turkey or ham, delicately layered, piled high and topped with slices of cheese and mustard. They had what I thought of as "curly" meat. I didn't know about fresh sliced meat from the grocer's deli section and wondered where white people got that "curly" meat, the kind they layered and easily folded in an S-shape between bread slices. They unscrewed bottles of Pepsi, as I recall, chilled and refreshing from their coolers. One mother accented her meal with a side of potato salad. Meanwhile, even the white bread on my sandwich seemed inferior, thin and flimsy looking now. My bologna and pop had warmed in the tin box, and I sensed everyone eyeing my lukewarm meal, pitying the super-value look of it. I did not enjoy my sandwich that day. I wished we were back in the school cafeteria, eating square pizza or even runny macaroni and cheese. I ate quickly. I crumpled up that stiff wax paper and that cheap Faygo soda can, and I tossed them into the trash, hoping to remove their low-class stain.

I was a top student; teachers scribbled "Excellent!" on my spelling and math tests, with shiny stickers and smiley faces at the top of graded assignments. I did not get detention slips for talking out of turn or getting in trouble. Stephanie and Lisa were also good students. Yet this field trip highlighted our differences. Afterward, my relationship with them changed in ways I couldn't articulate back then. Now I knew, without doubt, that we existed in very different worlds. We all knew it. Our mothers did not talk on the phone, like Stephanie's and Lisa's apparently did. There would be no sleepovers at each other's home. I lived, literally, on the other side of the train tracks and somehow—in the time it took to eat a bologna sandwich—I felt my identity diminish. I did not belong there, under the pavilion with Stephanie and Lisa and their mothers. *Good Times* collided with *The Brady Bunch* in real life. I wondered if white girls and their mothers everywhere were eating thick turkey and Swiss cheese sandwiches, thinking they were better than me.

Racial lines appeared more fiercely as I grew older. Once, a white man chased my sister and me out of a clothing store. We had a go-to spot to shop for cheap new outfits, a now-defunct franchise called Fashion Mine. We'd shopped there for years, or at least since both of us had started earning money to shop and Deborah had gotten her own car. By this time, she had graduated high school and was taking college classes part-time while working in the office of a national trucking company based in Fort Wayne. Still in high school, I saved up my allowance or, later, my check from cashiering at a grocery store to buy fast-food burgers, banana shakes, and cheap clothes. At Fashion Mine, I could buy a cute shirt from the clearance rack for ten or fifteen dollars, plus matching earrings. Deborah and I shared clothes, even though I stand a good five inches taller. Off to Northcrest Shopping Center we went, a popular spot for the whole family.

My father bought most appliances and electrical devices at the anchor store, Montgomery Ward. Fashion Mine stood nearby in the strip mall.

Our typical shopping strategy started with the clearance racks at the back of the store, so that's where we headed. I didn't really need anything but thought I might find a new top or pair of crop pants to sport at North Side High. I was filing through hangers on a sale rack when Deborah whispered, "He's following us."

I looked up to notice an older man working that evening. I hadn't seen him before. Women usually worked in the store, so he might have been a new employee or a manager. He traced our every move, shadowing just a few feet behind. We kept shopping, or at least pretending to shop at this point, separating the hangers, pulling out a blouse and holding it up for consideration. Then we'd walk across the store and stop at another rack to see if he followed along. He did. It was the proverbial tale of the white person following Black customers in a retail store—the story that so many African Americans can tell. Only this felt worse. He didn't try to hide it. He wanted us to see him seeing us.

I had not felt prejudice so intensely in a retail setting before. In my younger years, we walked to the neighborhood candy store down the street from our house to buy pieces of penny candy, Tootsie Rolls and sweet tarts and such. The owners were Black, and customers came from the neighborhood. My mother had warned of white people tailing Blacks in stores, but now I experienced it firsthand. Deborah and I talked loudly, letting the man know that we knew his strategy. "Is he following us?" we said, although we already knew the answer. "He must think we're going to steal something." We glanced at him, and he glared back. He did not want us there. We headed for the door.

Over her shoulder, Deborah said, "You're so busy watching the Blacks, the real thieves are stealing right under your nose."

This angered him somehow, and he sped up, huffing and breathing hard on our heels. My heart beat hard. *Is he going to get us?* We walked faster, out the door, scampering to the parking lot. He didn't let up. We reached Deborah's car and finally felt safe enough to look back. There he stood at the door, waving his fist at us and yelling something that I don't remember because, by now, fear made it hard to listen.

We rode away shaken and confused. Was it just our skin color that convinced him we intended to steal? Had other African Americans come to the store that he suspected, and he thought we were the same people? Had someone robbed the store, and he assumed two young Black girls must be to blame? Later we told our mother, but she wasn't surprised. "White people think Black people steal," she said matter-of-factly.

I never went back to Fashion Mine, and the store went out of business some years later. I wish I could say I based my decision on principle, not wanting to spend money in a place where workers treated me so badly, but the truth is, the man spooked me. I didn't know what might happen if I dared walk through those doors again. Next time, would he chase me all the way to the car?

The anxiety of getting got by angry white people implanted itself and stayed within me for a long time, throughout high school and into college. In high school, I wrote stories for the yearbook staff and knew I wanted to be a newspaper reporter. The Ernie Pyle School of Journalism at Indiana University (IU) would be a great start to my career. My older brother had attended IU, and the school accepted me several years later. Our family learned from his experience and folklore that making the three-hour trip to southern Indiana held potential dangers of its own, largely because reaching the Bloomington campus required driving through Martinsville.

The small Indiana town became a touchpoint for fear among African Americans after someone stabbed and murdered twenty-one-year-old Carol Jenkins-Davis, a Black woman selling encyclopedias one evening door-to-door. That happened in 1968. Martinsville gained a reputation as one of the many racist cities in Indiana, right along with official "sundown towns" across the United States, where Black people dared not travel at night. Sundown towns were hailed as such because of their policies and, in many cases, frank signs that read: "Nigger, Don't Let the Sun Go Down on You in [name of city]." Other cities in Indiana carried the label, including Goshen, which passed a resolution acknowledging and denouncing its past sundown town status in 2015. Whether Martinsville ever had an official sign shooing Blacks away is unclear, but African American IU students knew better than to take a chance there.

My brother witnessed the racism firsthand. In 1984, he and other members of North Side High School's track team journeyed to IU, where the college hosted an annual invitational track meet for high school teams throughout the state. Arbra often competed in the long jump and a relay race. After a long day, the team needed to grab dinner before completing the drive home. The bus stopped at a McDonald's in Martinsville. Arbra and a couple others finished their burgers and walked in a cluster back to the bus. The atmosphere in the parking lot had changed from when they'd first arrived. As the sun set, the lot filled with muscle cars, Dodges and such with their engines roaring. The scene mirrored something out of the old 1980s TV series *Dukes of Hazzard*, where white brothers drove around in a car called the "General Lee," its hood emblazoned with a Confederate flag. In Martinsville, the McDonald's obviously equaled a Saturday night hangout for young whites with adrenaline and fast cars. One of them screeched and stopped alongside my brother's group. White boys packed the interior, four or five deep. An overweight driver loomed huge behind the wheel, Arbra recalls.

"You niggers don't hurry up and get on that bus and get out of town, I'm gonna back this car up and run your asses over," he said. "And we know the sheriff, and he's not gonna do a damn thing about it."

No longer middle school boys scurrying to school, Arbra and his friends didn't run away or back down, instead unleashing choice cuss words of their own. But by now, one of the coaches noticed the standoff and ordered the students to get back on the bus. They told him what happened, but not much came of it, at least not from what Arbra could see. He vaguely recalls some words of encouragement, like "Don't pay any attention to them."

Once on the bus, they didn't stay on the subject long. My brother didn't mention it to our parents or the family once home. There was no scene with our father arriving from the factory and sitting on Arbra's bed with words of wisdom. No, the interaction felt too familiar, just a resurgence of his earlier school days. "We had encountered racism and stuff like that from white boys before, back at Lakeside," he says.

Today, he says the incident didn't affect him much. "It was just another experience for me. It wasn't something that had the bite or depth as it does when you get older, and you look back and you're like, 'Wow.'" Now he understands the deep, unprovoked hatred toward him behind those experiences.

Just a toddler when James Earl Ray assassinated Martin Luther King Jr., my brother says he somehow remembers it—not the actual details or the political implications, but he recalls images of King flooding the television, the angst of the traumatic time somehow embedding itself within his two-year-old frame. The dream of equality had not been realized, and racial hatred paraded itself openly. That's why people didn't always react to racial confrontations back then. "It was such a common thing, just coming out of that period," he says. "We just looked at it as another incident. . . . We understood it for what it was."

And what, exactly, was it?

"That's just white people being white people," he says.

Yet he had white friends, plenty of them. In middle school, he ran from the white guy in the Charger in the Lakeside neighborhood. Yet, he'd ride his bike to the nearby Forest Park area, where white friends invited him to play basketball outside their big houses, the kind of homes that tossed mini candy bars into Halloween baskets. He played sports with them, ran track. As a teenager, he dated a white classmate, whose father found their love letters and beat her for dating a Black guy. Racial perspectives differed, he knew, even within families.

"I didn't look at all whites as being the same," he says. "I didn't take those experiences and hold all white people accountable, because I knew all white people weren't like that."

Yet, Arbra never forgot that driver in the McDonald's parking lot, recounting his threat word for word nearly four decades later: *You niggers don't hurry up and get on that bus and get out of town, I'm gonna back this car up and run your asses over. And we know the sheriff . . .*

"Incidents like that—they stick out in your mind," he says. "I'll never forget that."

When Arbra went off to Indiana University and then I went off to IU, we scheduled trips to avoid driving through Martinsville after dark. The same held true for most African Americans we knew on campus in the early 1980s and 1990s. Years later, I would read an *Indianapolis Star* article about how Martinsville wanted to shed its racist image, about how some white residents there never knew the stigma existed when they'd moved to southern Indiana. I read about Kenneth Richmond, the man eventually arrested and charged in 2002 with killing Jenkins-Davis. He had ties to the Klan but actually lived elsewhere, in Hendricks County, where he worked on a farm. Martinsville residents said their city bore the racist stigma unfairly. In 2017, the mayor took a step toward shedding the shame by dedicating a memorial stone in Jenkins-Davis's honor and placing it at the entrance to the municipal building. During a special ceremony, Martinsville residents joined hands and prayed, along with members of Jenkins-Davis's family, who'd traveled to be there. About 150 people attended, according to the *Indianapolis Star*.

In 2019, I traveled back to IU for the first time in twenty-five years for a reunion of my peers who served on a student assembly called the Union Board. We worked together for two years, governing a portion of the college's funding to create and host different programs for the student body and to experience leadership ourselves. I left Fort Wayne a few hours later than originally planned that day, hurriedly making my way south on Interstate 69 to Bloomington. I didn't have a chance to eat much, so a couple of hours into the three-hour drive, I felt the hunger pangs. I wanted to stop and get a quick sandwich, and I looked for an exit with fast food. Highway signs said that the next exit would put me in Martinsville. By now the sun was setting, and something inside of me tightened. So many years removed from my college travel strategy, thoughts of this tiny town hadn't resurfaced until now. In an instant, fear crept in.

I debated with myself about the silliness of it all. A grown woman in my forties, I had dealt with threats and danger, perceived and real. I traveled various parts of the country, knocking on the doors of strangers with a reporter's notepad in my hand. I opened a racist letter from a reader once, calling me a nigger because of an article I'd written—a letter that swiftly went into the trash without much thought. I had flown thirteen hours over the Atlantic to the United Arab Emirates for my birthday, walked the streets carefully, discreetly wearing a hijab while touring one city governed by the male-dominated laws of Saudi Arabia. During a mission trip to Uganda, I had gripped the edges of a small boat tossed to and fro by the merciless rapids of the Nile River.

Nevertheless, I now gripped the steering wheel of my own car, scared of what might happen if I pumped my brakes in a little southern Indiana town. *Of course, I should stop,* I told myself. *I'm hungry, and I have the right to buy food at a restaurant like anyone else.* Besides, the Martinsville of the twenty-first century had likely outgrown its old reputation, I reasoned. Of course, it had.

Still, I did not stop. I couldn't. I kept driving straight to the sanctuary of campus, where I'd once used my position on the Union Board to rally for diversity and acceptance among student groups. I checked into my hotel room. Then, stomach growling, I walked in the darkness of night along a bustling thoroughfare lined with bars and restaurants, surrounded by college students and alumni.

Counselors and other experts say trauma is something that sticks with you, that it can even be passed down from one generation to the next through DNA. They speak of microaggressions, those common negative attitudes and stigmas against people of color that can eventually tear down self-esteem and create stress and fear where there need be none. I had read about racial trauma and thought about its enduring power, but on that drive it hit me: the trauma of racism had lived beyond articles and textbooks; it was lodged somewhere deep inside of me too. I didn't know if it had grabbed hold with that lunch at the zoo or the incident at Fashion Mine or with the fear of traveling through certain places because of my skin color. Perhaps, it was a combination of all those things and more, so much more. And maybe it had begun decades before I was even born. Maybe it implanted itself in my mother, as she experienced the hatred of the South, especially when justice failed her father. It could be, I thought, that the trauma of racism had wedged in our bones, having been passed down from one generation to the next, right alongside the faith we needed to overcome it.

CHAPTER TEN

—⁓—

A BLACK MAN'S CAPITAL CRIME

IN 1957, THE LEGAL TEAM of Fitts and Locke had to balance their time between Granddaddy's case and at least one more prominent legal proceeding. That year, they joined up to fight for Jimmy Wilson, a fifty-five-year-old "illiterate Negro" and ex-felon now charged with a fresh crime. Not that they volunteered for the job. Wilson lacked an attorney and money to pay for one. A judge appointed the duo to represent him in a case that reached far beyond Alabama into the North and even overseas. Actually, Jimmy Wilson would take the names of Fitts and Locke all over the world in ways Alabamans never imagined.

His offense? Wilson, a handyman, stole $1.95 from an eighty-two-year-old woman's home in Marion, Alabama. The elderly woman also said Wilson choked her and tried to rape her. Wilson eventually admitted to taking the coins but strongly denied ever touching the woman, and prosecutors never pursued assault or attempted rape charges. Instead, they charged him with robbery, which meant he took the money "by force of fear or threat of violence," and that was enough. In 1957, Alabama considered robbery a capital crime, at least for accused Negroes. Reports reveal that only four people had been sentenced to death in Alabama for robbery at the time, all of them Negroes. Jurors convicted Wilson, and for this two-dollar theft, he got the electric chair.

Fitts and Locke argued in Wilson's defense during the automatic appeal process. They objected to the elderly woman's testimony on the stand because her words veered from the financial loss to talk of attempted rape—a serious allegation against a Negro in the South but one for which prosecutors didn't bother to file charges in this case. Fitts and Locke called her testimony prejudicial and the punishment excessive. Yet the Alabama Supreme Court upheld the

76

death penalty, and Wilson's execution date loomed, to the shock of northerners and the rest of the civilized world.

Gov. James Folsom's office stayed busy, as thousands of letters poured in daily protesting the execution. Opponents wanted a pardon. Envelopes included petitions with as many as 4,500 signatures. People sent personal checks for $1.95. Shortly before the execution date, US secretary of state John Foster Dulles wired a report to Gov. Folsom, recounting reaction overseas. The American embassy in London received about 650 letters and telegrams in protest, including schools, churches, and labor unions. Outcries bellowed from Ireland, Canada, Trinidad, Jamaica, Germany, France, and Belgium. Further, people in Brazil circulated petitions, and a representative to the United Nations from the Uruguayan embassy had been instructed to convey "solicitude for clemency." The case embarrassed the United States globally during its Cold War with Russia and revealed the nation's hypocrisy. Americans touted their democracy as the ideal for other countries to follow and as superior to communism while oppressing their own Black citizens and condemning a man to death for less than two dollars.

Despite the defense by Fitts and Locke, some doubted their effectiveness in representing a Negro, perhaps even more so since they were court appointees ordered to take the case in the first place. By this time, Thurgood Marshall and the National Association for the Advancement of Colored People (NAACP) had made a name for themselves, stepping in on high-profile cases for Negro justice. Marshall led the charge in *Brown v. Board of Education* and fought against injustices that fatally doomed men like Wilson. Negroes across the country sought help from the NAACP.

Much of that activity halted in Alabama, though. The state had banned the NAACP from operating within its borders, so justice for Wilson there seemed a long shot. State attorney general John Patterson filed a lawsuit against the NAACP a year earlier, in 1956, alleging that the group harmed Alabamans by promoting such activities as the Montgomery bus boycott and forcing the admission of a Black student, Autherine Lucy, to the University of Alabama. Patterson argued that these developments shined negative publicity on their fair state and put Alabama in a distasteful light. The suit maneuvered several court proceedings, including decisions passed down from the US Supreme Court. Finally, in 1964, the NAACP would again operate in Alabama. Several incremental court decisions declared that the First Amendment protected the organization's activities as free speech and the right for likeminded people to organize in groups.

That decision came much too late for Wilson. The NAACP couldn't step in to help in 1957. Yet, after Fitts and Locke apparently felt they could do no more, a budding Black civil rights attorney named Fred Gray took up the case, although not officially under the NAACP's umbrella. Gray had already defended Rosa Parks, after police arrested her for refusing to give up her seat on a bus in Montgomery. He would go on to represent Martin Luther King Jr. and the NAACP in its fight to operate in Alabama. In this case, Gray headed to the governor with a plea for mercy on Jimmy Wilson's behalf. During a forty-minute clemency hearing, Gray argued that execution under the circumstances would be "an inhuman act." He said the original jury would never have deemed Wilson worthy of death if he were white. Two of Wilson's brothers also asked the governor for mercy. The clemency hearing, the international pressure, and Gov. Folsom's known distaste for the death penalty likely all worked together to make a difference. Finally, in the fall of 1958, the governor commuted Wilson's sentence to life imprisonment. He would do prison time for the crime but not lose his life.

I weaved together facts about Jimmy Wilson and other Fitts activities to create a clearer picture of my grandfather's attorney. During one of my trips to the Dallas County Courthouse, I traveled the back roads of Uniontown, Browns, and Marion where Fitts had lived. I hoped to connect with his family there, namely a son, Sheldon Fitts Jr. The same weekend I found Robert Radford, I also looked up the younger Fitts by scrolling and cold-calling names in my hotel room phone book.

I repeated my spiel to Fitts Jr., adding that his father had represented my grandfather in a 1950s civil lawsuit. I asked if he had any of his father's old files. He didn't, but he loosened up enough to give some information about the family. They were dairy farmers, Fitts Jr. explained by phone. He was in high school, working on the farm, when his father did legal work.

"Dad was a good lawyer," he said. "He was a fine person, and he always treated people right and tried to do what was right in his lifetime."

I delved deeper, hoping for insight into Fitts Sr.'s views on race. At the time, I envisioned Sheldon Fitts the lawyer falling on the side of history that crusaded for Negroes' rights. I told his son that the story went beyond the car accident for which my grandfather had hired his father. My grandfather was a Black man, I said, and he'd been kidnapped by white men who didn't want him to collect in the case. But rather than open a door for deeper conversation, my details had the opposite effect.

"I'd rather not talk about it," Fitts Jr. said now. "It's a lot of history, and Dad's dead and gone." (Fitts Sr. died in 1987.)

"But your father did such a good thing," I pleaded.

Fitts Jr. said he was young during that time and not at all involved in his father's legal work, so he really had nothing to add. He reiterated something about not wanting to go back to those days and bring up the past. I asked if I could call him at another time, perhaps, giving him space to think more about the situation.

"I'm very busy," he said.

His tone was soft but firm. He couldn't be cajoled, at least not now. I gave him my cell phone number to call if he changed his mind, but I wouldn't bet on him having written it down. Later, back in Florida, I sent him a letter, asking again for an interview. He never responded.

In retrospect, I was naïve to think the son of my grandfather's lawyer might invite me to his home to sip sweet iced tea and talk for hours about his father's quest for justice. I wanted to take him back to a time when America accepted and, in many areas, embraced blatant racism as the norm—a time that most white people avoid discussing, even today. I don't know why Sheldon Fitts Jr. didn't want to talk more. I do know that, in many ways, race relations are as complicated in the United States in the twenty-first century as they were in the 1950s. Back then, just like today, America struggled with its identity as a so-called melting pot and land of liberty, while also being a nation where people of color are disqualified, oppressed, and not treated equally.

From my own research, I gained some understanding of Fitts Sr. Like most whites in the South at the time, the lawyer born in 1899 was a staunch Democrat and proudly so. One of his political ads for circuit solicitor touted, "Is now & always has been a Democrat. I am obligated to no one." Back then the Democratic Party represented different values than it does today. Before the civil rights movement, southern Democrats argued staunchly for the separation of the races. Remember, Abraham Lincoln fought against slavery—but as a Republican. After emancipation forced plantation owners to set slaves free, Negroes enjoyed a short-lived semblance of progress in the South during the Reconstruction era. Some owned property and served in political offices in Alabama. But a massive push by southern Democrats and an active Ku Klux Klan ended all that, establishing the false "separate but equal" policies and Jim Crow. By the time Fitts Sr. was born, Negroes had overcome slavery, but not their inferior status politically, socially, and economically. (One political party couldn't contain Klan members, however. Some labeled themselves Democrats, while others called themselves Republican, and they lived all over the nation, not just in the South.)

Fitts fit snugly into the segregationist mindset of early and mid-twentieth-century Democrats, especially those in the South. Some claimed to have no problem with Negroes—they just didn't want to be around them much. Others proved proud racists and Klan members. Still others didn't don white costumes but went so far as to fight for racial separation in schools, housing, restaurants, or wherever they lived out their own lives. Status was important, too. Black men and women could take low-wage jobs in white owners' fields and as maids in their homes, as long as they stayed in their place.

Right around this time, the major political parties began to redefine themselves. Some long-term southern Democrats got fed up with their party's support for President Roosevelt's New Deal programs, intended to give relief during the Great Depression. The programs effectively expanded the federal government's role, and some initiatives lingered long after the Depression, even to this day, such as social security and a form of the welfare program that Granddaddy and Big Mama used to get by.

Mary D. Cain reigned prominently among those redefining Democrats, someone whose views Fitts would come to idealize. The owner of the *Summit Sun* newspaper and the first female candidate to run for governor of Mississippi, Cain campaigned on the Democratic ticket, the same party as presidents Roosevelt and Harry Truman after him. Yet some called her "the New Deal's worst enemy." Cain stood firmly against initiatives that gave the federal government more power than the states, opposing Prohibition, the New Deal, and civil rights. She called social security unconstitutional and un-American, gaining national attention when she refused to pay a self-employment tax. In response, the Internal Revenue Department put a padlock on the door of her newspaper offices, which she swiftly cut off with a hacksaw. That earned her national acclaim and the nickname "Hacksaw Mary."

Hacksaw lost her 1951 and 1955 gubernatorial bids but remained a booming political voice in the South. As party allegiances shifted, Cain gave speeches in 1952 favoring the Republican Eisenhower-Nixon presidential ticket against Democrat Adlai Stevenson. An Alabama radio station scheduled one of Cain's pro-Eisenhower speeches for just days before the 1952 presidential election. Pumped by Cain's political banter, Fitts Sr. encouraged others in his native and nearby Chilton County to tune in. According to a report in the *Union-Banner*, "Hon. Sheldon Fitts, attorney of Marion, former Chilton County citizen, says to his Chilton friends: 'This is one of the finest speeches I have ever heard; I hope the people of Chilton county will hear these broadcasts.'"

Cain's positions on the issues reveal the complexities of prejudice and discrimination then and now. She argued against integration and programs beneficial to economically depressed Negroes. Yet she called herself a friend to Blacks. Her newspaper featured a column devoted to news particular to the Negro community in Summit, Mississippi. The paper also included pictures

of Blacks and referred to them with courtesy titles, such as "Mr." and "Mrs."—
"an unusual practice for a white-owned southern newspaper in this period,"
according to the Mississippi Encyclopedia.

Cain spoke her mind clearly in a 1966 NBC documentary on race called
Mississippi: A Self Portrait. "I think Mississippi has done wonders with our race
relations," she said, wearing pearls, a beehive hairdo, and a proud smile for the
camera. She continued:

> I think it has been a marvelous thing that our Negroes have come as far
> as they have. And I feel no sense of guilt and I do not feel that we need
> to apologize for what we have done for them. And I feel that God had a
> purpose in creating the races separately. I am so proud of Negroes who are
> proud of being Negroes. They are what God made them. And I'm proud of
> being white because I am what my white race has made me. I'm white today
> because my parents practiced segregation. And I wouldn't be anything but
> white. And I love Negroes who wouldn't be anything but Negro.

When I contrast Cain's seeming respect for Negroes on one hand and her
fight to maintain segregation on the other, I see how deeply prejudice buries
itself within the soul. So deep, in fact, that she and others could act as though
they appreciated Negroes while blatantly disrespecting and stifling their social and economic progress. The contradiction didn't end with hers and Fitts's
generation. Today, what people say about racial harmony never quite tells the
whole story; nor does their job, title, or political affiliation. How they really feel
often comes out in one-on-one discussions and in the policies they support or
decry.

An intense conversation I had once with a colleague is a case in point of
how racial views are deep-seated. This colleague's job revolved around serving
under-resourced people and improving their health. She spent a career saying all the right things about the lack of services available to the nation's most
vulnerable. She'd donated to worthy causes. Still, none of those speeches or
presentations represented her genuine views on service and equality. I learned
as much when she initiated a conversation about the Affordable Care Act
(ACA), also known as "Obamacare," just after Donald Trump won the presidential election. Talk swirled nationally about whether Trump would end the
comprehensive health reform legislation designed to increase coverage for the
uninsured, as many Republican leaders vowed to do. My colleague vigorously
opposed universal healthcare and, apparently, sought to prove her stance legiti-
mate to a Black woman, such as myself. She'd heard stories about middle-class
Americans who now had to pay higher insurance premiums, she said. Plus, the

ACA restricted their choices for doctors. These were valid points, and I agreed that elected officials needed to work to improve the legislation, but I argued that they should not repeal it. "What about those in the low-income bracket and people with serious preexisting conditions?" I asked her. They now had access to the health care they desperately needed. Besides, these were the people whose needs she rallied to serve day in and day out. She agreed health care was good for them, too, but she didn't buy the idea that others should adjust their lives or sacrifice personally to make it happen.

What an aha moment for me. Some white Americans, I realized, can be so-called allies for people of color on a surface level by simply *talking* about their issues. They acknowledge societal wrongs, appearing learned and compassionate at work, at church, in meetings. But those same people could dismiss Blacks' and Latinos' needs on a deeper level that required not just talk but personal sacrifice. In other words, they drew a hard line when rallying for Blacks' rights required action that threatened their own white privilege. Through the lens of history, Cain fit that mold, a woman who took pride in calling Negroes "Mr." and "Mrs." on the pages of her newspaper, but who opposed their full rights in society. Integration would risk the comfortable and prestigious white life and norms she knew. Like the modern service provider who opposed universal health care, a segregationist in the 1950s would have viewed integration as a costly inconvenience, a sacrifice for whites, and, apparently, a bridge too far. The issue, I've come to realize, is not what people are willing to *give* in the name of justice but what they are willing to *give up*.

Of course, Mary Cain and Sheldon Fitts were two different people with two different minds. Their views on race may have been quite similar, though. One article I found from the *Arkansas State Press* tells me as much, at least when I consider Cain's muddied perspective on racism, what she called being a "friend" to Negroes, and Fitts's enthusiasm for her political rhetoric. The Black-owned newspaper was among many nationwide that followed the Jimmy Wilson story. Negroes kept up with the latest developments in the case of the handyman and petty thief on death row. Just as they did in Granddaddy's case, some wondered if the white attorneys, Fitts and Locke, did all they could for true justice. Those who read the *Arkansas State Press* may have gotten their answer. Before the governor pardoned Wilson, the paper ran a bold, politically incorrect headline: "'That Nigger Was Lucky He Wasn't Lynched,' Says Defense Attorney." The attorney referenced in the headline is Sheldon Fitts Sr. The article describes how he and some other Alabama officials seemed shocked by the international interest in Wilson's case.

Wilson "got off well" with a scheduled execution, the article says Fitts told reporters. "That nigger was lucky he wasn't lynched," he said, after Fred Gray took over the case. Fitts explained the way these things worked in Alabama, noting that state law deemed robbery a capital offense. Nothing more could be done, he said, the law being clear and the sentence being rendered. Southern officials close to the case, including Prison Warden Steve Nixon, insisted Wilson had already accepted his fate and awaited death "calmly" at Atmore prison farm. The public uproar baffled them.

"You people north of the Mason-Dixon line are sure to have everything wrong again," Fitts said, according to the article. During the appeal, Fitts argued against the elderly woman's attempted rape testimony, calling it prejudicial. But now, away from the courts, he said, "There's no doubt that this nigger did it. He tried to rape this feeble old white lady. . . . You people are good intending folks," Fitts is quoted as saying, "but you should come down here and see the niggers we got. We don't hate our niggers down here. Why, I loved my old nigger mammy and I have some good friends who are niggers. It's just that we got our place and they got theirs."

—⚭—

CHAPTER ELEVEN

HE WAS "THAT"

DURING THE THIRTEEN-MINUTE drive across Fort Wayne to Frank Page's house, I mentally listed some general questions to ask as a framework for my interview. Relatives warned that he talked a lot, so I wouldn't need to prime him much. What a shame I'd never exchanged words with Granddaddy's brother, the only sibling still alive in early 2020. Technically, they were half brothers. After Granddaddy's mother died, his father remarried, and the new couple had children together. In total, Granddaddy had about thirteen siblings. They named the youngest boy Frank, which somehow evolved through the years to Papa Page for some and Pop Page or simply Pop for many others.

He lived now with his wife, Lola, a spry, friendly woman with smooth shiny cheeks and a voice that carried. She greeted me at the door and invited me to a seat on the living room couch. "Frank!" she yelled toward a short hallway that led to back rooms. "You got company."

Ms. Lola, as I took to calling her, made sure I felt comfortable and knew the history of her and Frank's family, while we waited for him to appear. They'd spent more than fifty years together—both had lost track of the exact number now. Framed eight-by-tens covered walls, shelves, and tabletops throughout the room. Their children's graduations, weddings, and family gatherings created a wallpaper effect. Ms. Lola went over them, pointing out highlights of each occasion. Several had moved far away, as children do when they grow up, she lamented.

Another twenty minutes passed before she yelled toward the back room again. "Frank? She might have something else to do," Ms. Lola said, referring to me. He didn't say anything, but soon a thumping sound hit the carpet.

Frank Page. *Courtesy of Lola Page*

Slowly, he emerged maneuvering a walker as it thumped ahead and steadied him. He tilted his head upward with that grin of his and made eye contact. Lola introduced me.

"This is your brother's granddaughter," she said, reminding him of our earlier phone conversation to set up my visit.

"Oh yeah?" He paused, looked at me from the side and smiled. "That's Book's granddaughter," he said, using one of the nicknames family called Granddaddy because he liked to read.

Frank idled farther into the living room, pushing his walker forward, then taking two steps and pushing his walker again. A smile dominated his face the whole time, not that it was particularly wide or toothy. It just radiated somehow. The kind that makes a stranger think he might be the nicest man you've met in a long time. His eyes, though, tunneled deep, like he'd seen a forever's worth of trouble in his eighty-nine years.

His voice flowed softly, barely above a whisper. By the doctors' accounts, he should've been dead and gone long ago, he told me. None of the illnesses over the years proved strong enough to claim his life, though. The throat cancer softened his sound a bit, but it couldn't hush him for good.

He sat beside me on the couch, and I started the conversation by showing him aged black-and-white photos of his other siblings. "That's LeRoy," he'd say. That's Bea. That's Sally Bell. At some point, he asked out of nowhere, "You seen Fat Pig?" He laughed. That's the nickname he coined for one of my uncles who used to catch a ride with him to the Zollner factory where both worked after migrating to Fort Wayne. "I call him that to his face," he said, cracking himself up.

After a while, I shifted the conversation. "Tell me about your life growing up."

Head tilted, he told me I didn't want to know, although we both knew the truth—I did want to know, and he wanted to tell me.

"At the time, I was *that*," he explained of his young years. He said this with a certain coyness. Seeing the question in my eyes, he went further. "If *it* was that, *I* was that."

"That," he said, referred to his bad-boy-ness, his lack of fear. Growing up, he didn't bow to rules or back down from adversity. Conflict only unleashed his inner fight, driving him to be as bad as the situation required. In other words, whatever force proved necessary for him to come out on top, he was *that*.

Before long, I knew relatives had told the truth when they'd called him a talker. I gave up on my questions, and the conversation flowed into a groove of its own. He'd tell me a story, or more likely one story that led to another story and another, before he circled back around to tie up the original story. I listened.

And Ms. Lola moved about the house, interjecting occasionally with an observation of her own. "I can't believe how they treated people back then," she said.

My great uncle expounded on his thatness. "I told my baby girl's boyfriend, 'If you do anything to her, you better do it to yourself, 'cause if I'm living, I might do a little worse.'"

Long before he stood as protective father in Indiana, people in Browns and Uniontown knew Frank Page was that, which is why they didn't tell him about Granddaddy's case, at least not right away. By the time the accident occurred in 1954, Frank's mother had already sent him packing to Fort Wayne. Given no choice, Frank either had to leave or die, possibly at the hands of a white man. He dropped slivers of this story that shuffled him north throughout our talk. He'd say the whole thing revolved around a couple bales of cotton. From what I could tell, it started way before then, just as all turning points in life do.

Granddaddy had already lived twenty-two years and had a wife and children of his own when Frank came to life in 1930. His closest friend was actually his nephew, one of Granddaddy's sons that Frank called by both his first name and middle initial, Langhorn B. He described his younger years with his siblings and Israel Sr., Frank and Granddaddy's father. The senior Israel wielded a lot of responsibility on the land where the Pages lived and multiplied. He managed the crops and other issues for W. T. Buck, who owned it. Buck, if you'll recall, later sold Granddaddy that old Chevy.

Legal slavery had ended nearly sixty years before Frank's childhood, but emancipation seemed a mere technicality to him. Negroes still had to live somewhere, and whites held onto the land, never turning over the promised forty acres. That meant the Negroes worked through sharecropping arrangements where they tended the fields, picking cotton and crops on land they didn't own. They didn't work for reasonable wages but rather for the right to simply exist on someone else's property, in some ways all too similar to the slavery they'd supposedly overcome.

"Like I tell my kids, the white man owned you, if he had money," Frank said. "You had to work for them. If you stayed on their place, you had to work for *them*."

Still, for a boy who didn't know the difference from Negro living and white living, life didn't seem worth complaining about, at least when Israel Sr. was alive and handled everything. Frank, his brothers, and his sisters lived in one house, while some of the older set of siblings—those from Israel Sr.'s first marriage, including Granddaddy—lived in other houses nearby.

"I can remember all of them living there," Frank said of the older set. They shared a mule, and Israel Sr. coordinated their work. He managed how they tilled the land and picked the cotton and made their way. He kept the books for Buck, writing entries with flowing handwriting that impressed Frank, even as a little boy.

"And he had a lot up here," Frank said, pointing to his temple, "upstairs."

Israel Sr. took his older sons into the woods and showed them how to cut trees, fashion logs, stack them this way and that to build a house that could stand during the storms. Listening to Frank, I saw Israel Sr. as a soft-hearted man, and I believe that's where Granddaddy got a lot of his ways. For one, Israel Sr. never spanked the kids, Frank said, only their mother did that. And he'd plead with her to let them be. Another thing, he was a smart man, especially when it came to managing things. The same way people described Granddaddy.

They say Israel Sr. died of a heart attack or stroke. Whatever the cause, Frank was only nine years old when they buried him. The family's circumstances turned sour after that. Like most women at the time, Frank's mother, Corinne, couldn't provide for all the kids she and Israel Sr. had together. The siblings split up for a time to live with different relatives. Frank stayed with his mother's father, Floyd Hood, also known as "Top Hood." Mr. Hood, Frank said, held the rarest of occupations for a Negro—a doctor. As Frank tells it, folks lined up outside Top Hood's house for treatment. Frank spent several years there, before moving back to Corinne's, where he continued being that. On a given weekend, he'd be drinking moonshine with Langhorn B., pulling pranks, and eyeing women. The older he got, the more trouble found him, often with the ladies.

As a matter of fact, Frank got the worst beating of his life on account of a woman. Her name was Rosa Lee, as he recalled. She'd come to town, visiting from big-city New York, so she sparked a lot of curiosity with the young men in Browns. Corinne had given Frank two silver dollars to go uptown and buy some fish. It was a Friday, and they always ate fish every Friday. ("And he still do," Lola interjected.) But all the way to town, Frank's mind stayed on that gal from New York. He met up with her and, instead of buying fish for dinner, bought candy, cigarettes for twenty cents, and a whole lot of nothing. "It was fun after that," he said. Until he got back home with no food to show for his mother's money. Corinne made sure he never forgot it. "That was the worst whupping I ever got," he said.

For a while, he lived near Birmingham, where his older brothers worked at a steel mill. Frank wasn't supposed to work there; he was too young at sixteen. He didn't even weigh the required 150 pounds. For twenty bucks, he got a man to fill out the application and lie for him. A lot of teenagers did that, he said, and the bosses knew about it. They didn't mind hiring boys, especially from the country. "If you come off the farm, they know you'll work," Frank said. But the higher-ups found out before long and kicked him out of the plant. He went back to Corinne's house and picked cotton.

He never enjoyed cotton picking, not that anyone really finds pleasure in such work, but Frank just couldn't stand it, especially as a child. He'd bargain to stay home and babysit, at least when Israel Sr. lived. After he died, Corinne moved from Buck's land, and the new landlord had other people who used tractors to plow the farm and to keep the cotton clean. She and the kids did their best to pay off their rent by picking crops in the field. In time, only Frank, his mother, and his sister Pearl lived in the home. That made him the man of the house, and during his last year in Alabama, he worked hard to do right by his family.

Farming felt much different now with a single mother. "We didn't have no mules, no chickens, no hogs, nothing," he said. They had the right to pick cotton, and that was about it. Then everything fell apart over about two bales of the stuff. That's how much the family picked once, he said, a stellar feat, considering a bale generally weighed five hundred pounds. Pride swelled in him, and, knowing Frank, he didn't keep it to himself. This pride wasn't simply for pride's sake. That much cotton meant a big payout for his mother and his sister, even after the landowner got his share. They usually earned ten to fifteen dollars or so after turning in their raw cotton, compared to the undoubted hundreds that landowners took in. Frank didn't know exactly how much they'd get this time, but he waited eagerly to find out. They could stop worrying about surviving and maybe get ahead. Frank had to go to the landowner's office uptown to retrieve the family's cut. He put on his hat, caught the train, and walked through downtown till he came to the familiar building next to the drugstore. He'd done it so many times; the routine came easily.

"They didn't allow you to come in the office in the front," he said about Negroes. "You had to go up the back way. And I went up there, upstairs, right there in Uniontown."

Frank walked up the back stairwell, and the landowner opened the door.

"When I got in," he said, "Bam!" Frank felt a sharp thud to his head. "He hit me so hard my hat jumped off."

"Look up!" the man demanded.

Frank looked up.

"You see a roof?" the man asked rhetorically. "You see a ceiling on there? . . . You don't go in no building with your hat on."

Stunned, Frank got himself together a bit, picked up his cap, tried to keep his mind on the only thing that mattered anyway, the reason he had come.

"What about my money—for two bales of cotton?"

The man looked at Frank and smirked, like something was funny. Actually, there would be no compensation, he told Frank. No money for Frank and Corinne and his sister Pearl to get by. "You just got out of debt," he said.

In other words, Frank worked hard in the fields to produce one of the biggest hauls the family had turned over, likely since Israel Sr. died. Yet they wouldn't even get a silver dollar to buy Friday's fish. They owed it all to him, the owner said, their unending debt for living on another man's property.

Frank left the office a little poorer than when he'd left home. It had cost him a dime to catch the train. Despite his self-confidence, Frank remained powerless in the South over a white man who took advantage of him, stole his labor. That day, he learned that a sharecropper amounted to a new-age slave. He lived and worked on the white man's land at the white man's will. Frank sat on that train and swallowed the indignity that many young African Americans face at some point in life, like a rite of passage to adulthood in America. This reckoning with racial humiliation often creeps up when least expected. It could happen subtly, while shopping or while eating a bologna sandwich with classmates at the zoo. It could happen blatantly, like a false arrest, getting passed over for a job, being denied fair wages, or, in Frank's case, receiving no wages at all. Now he would return to his mother's house, again with empty pockets but a much different story to tell. What he did next on that train ride home fell out of character for someone who lived his life being that. Frank held his head up as best he could, but he let the tears fall.

"And I never would forget it," he told me, the tinge of pain hovering some seventy years later. "I went back crying."

Tears turned to an anger that consumed him soon after. Frank knew what to do next. A Negro may not get justice, but he could get revenge. He took Corinne's gun, the one his grandfather had given the single mother for safety. He envisioned aiming it, pulling the trigger, giving that white man what he deserved. In the barrel of a gun, he found hope, the possibility of satisfaction from an entire system that had shamed him, mocked his determination and sweat, that swindled a man's hard-earned money with a grin.

In the end, Frank's own mouth presented the biggest stumbling block for his plan. He couldn't keep quiet about it. It didn't take long before Corinne found out. She could stop her son from doing something stupid in the short term, but not forever. She contacted his big sister Bea, who had already moved to Fort Wayne and married.

"Come get him," Corinne told Bea.

Frank had visited Bea and her family once before but didn't care much for the Midwest. He stayed a whole week, wishing all the while he could get back down south. "Too cold," he said. Now he didn't have a choice. He couldn't live in Corinne's house, not plotting to shoot a white man. He'd get the whole family killed. Before long, Bea and her husband drove south and then back again with Frank in the back seat, watching the rich Alabama landscape glide by his window.

That was sometime around 1951 or 1952. Like everything else, exact dates don't mean much to him these days. He was long gone and shivering from the cold winters and snow in Indiana by the time Granddaddy's accident and the kidnapping happened. Nobody told him about either, not right away, not with his temper. By the time he heard about it, the events of the time had traveled from person to person to person, jumbling the facts along the way. On a trip with Ms. Lola down south years later, they slowed down on the bridge near the woods where those kidnappers took Granddaddy. He told her the story, as best he could recall what he'd been told. I revealed details from my research that he heard for the first time.

By now we were nearing our fourth hour together, and I'd heard all kinds of roguishness growing up with him and Langhorn B., about the Klan riding on horseback down infamous "Nigger Street," where Negroes partied in juke joints; about settling into Fort Wayne; about warning his own daughter to avoid Martinsville at night on trips back and forth to IU. The brightness of a Sunday afternoon turned to night, so I shut down my laptop and rose to leave. I had stopped by to learn more about my grandfather and great-grandfather, but I found his story compelling, too. I would likely include his experience as a sharecropper in the book, I told him. His response shaped the most surprising moment of the evening. The straight-talking Frank hesitated.

"People down there still know who I am," he said.

Ms. Lola and I looked at each other, confused. I asked if he was afraid of the landowner or somebody else finding him, coming up to Fort Wayne to harm him.

He nodded, and Ms. Lola cut in. "That was so long ago; those people are all dead by now," she said, voicing my thoughts.

Unconvinced, he said something about relatives who still lived down there. They still carried the Page name and might become targets of retaliation. Ms. Lola kept looking at me with raised brows, then looking back at him. "How would they come up here to get you?" Then she'd turn to me. "Go on and put it in there," she said. "Go on, put it in there." He still looked worried. I told him I understood why he would hesitate, considering all that had happened to him. I would let him see what I wrote about him before the book was published, I said. That made him feel better.

I left, considering the complexities of Frank's outlook on what happened in Alabama so long ago and how he still felt unsafe, dogged by an oppressor who was likely long dead. In Frank—just like in me—I saw how a Black person's circumstances could change, how he could move far away, take ownership of his life, and start all over again. Yet the trauma of racism remains. I saw how fear could embed itself for years and years and years to come, creating our reality, no matter how unrealistic it sounded to someone else.

I was in the process of writing two and a half months after my visit, when my mother ended a phone call and announced with despair, "Papa Page is gone." As the obituary stated, "On Thursday, May 21, 2020, at home and surrounded by his family, God stretched His hand to Pops and he peacefully took hold of it and started his journey to live in our hearts forever."

—ꟺ—

FAKE PREACHERS AND WINDING ROADS

WITH THE JIMMY WILSON case off their hands, Fitts ramped up Granddad-dy's lawsuit. A year before they got him, Fitts filed an amended complaint on February 5, 1958. He asked for more money in damages and clarified points in the first complaint that Lee's attorney rebutted. Granddaddy would never drill wells again—this they knew since the surgery failed to restore his arm. Fitts increased the damages, suing for $15,000, the equivalent of about $147,000 today. Granddaddy would get a portion, one of my uncles said, while Fitts and Locke would get their pay from the settlement, too.

In the amended complaint, Fitts addressed the defense attorney Smith's critiques and highlighted that Lee "wantonly" caused or allowed the cruiser to collide with Granddaddy's car. Granddaddy traveled the intersection of Highway 5 and Interstate 80, "both of which are public highways in the County of Dallas, State of Alabama," the complaint read. In other words, Granddaddy had a right to be there, a point that Lee's side seemed to question.

This time, Lee and Smith cited fourteen counts of rebuttal, implying that Granddaddy's attorneys were wrong to call the accident both wanton (or malicious) and negligent at the same time. They contended that the complaint lacked facts to show Granddaddy sustained damage or injury due to Lee's negligence. They said no facts presented proved whether Lee "was actually operating the automobile at the time of the alleged accident or was merely a passenger."

Of course, evidence existed to prove Lee drove the car, plenty of evidence. The state highway patrol wrote a report faulting and fining him. Lee had already paid his fine—in the same courthouse where he now alleged his guilt couldn't be proven. He himself said he ran the stop sign during the Talladega County commission meetings to get damages for his brother, Sam. And newspaper articles named him as the driver. Fitts likely planned to present this proof during trial, sealing a sure victory. It's also possible that he was unaware of at least some evidence since the Internet did not exist back then and the activities took place hundreds of miles apart. Lee's side, obviously, knew it all, better than anyone. Perhaps they were buying time with their illogical responses or just trying to frustrate Granddaddy, hoping he would drop the complaint.

Granddaddy had already suffered so much, though. He'd lost his arm, lost his job, lost money, his means of supporting his family, and lost his car. He had nothing more to lose by moving forward with the case, nothing but time. The struggle was real. A square of cornbread with syrup equaled a meal at times. Other days, they called a sweet potato dinner or a serving of hominy.

"It was really bad," Willie James said. "Sometimes we didn't know where we were going to get a meal from."

To be clear, times had always been tight, but at least before the accident, the family knew the storm clouds would lift. A well-drilling job and a check would come, they'd be able to pay their own way, and a man could hold onto the pride of being a provider. Big Mama grew vegetables in a garden on the land, so they got by even after the accident. She raised chickens, too, and some days she'd go out to the coop, choose one, and chase it. She grabbed the chicken by the neck and swung it around. Once the neck broke, she prepped it for cooking.

During the lean times when Granddaddy couldn't work, Big Mama comforted the children old enough to understand poverty. Their religion provided the proper foresight. "God will make a way," Big Mama would say. Willie James remembers her saying that over and over. Granddaddy clung to the same faith. God would make a way, indeed. But how?

All around them, the world kept turning, and Negroes kept fighting for rights and privileges that whites took for granted. A combination of tactics and the times finally launched the civil rights era. Negroes kept demanding that officials honor the *Brown v. Board of Education* decision to end racial segregation in schools. New laws were one thing. Compliance among local leaders and lawmakers equaled quite another. The Montgomery bus boycott made national headlines. After 381 days of Negroes boycotting buses, a federal court decision deemed forced segregation on buses unconstitutional. The US Supreme Court upheld the decision, and the boycott ended in December 1956. Yet other parts of the state kept right on forcing Negroes to sit in the back and give up their seats for whites.

Once, on a trip to Birmingham, my mother and her sisters sat in the designated rear of the bus when chaos broke out. A group of young Black girls and boys staged a sit-in, getting aboard and positioning themselves snuggly upfront with the white riders. My mother doesn't remember the outcome, only the initial ruckus and the fear she and my aunts felt. In 1957, President Eisenhower sent federal troops to escort nine Black students into Central High School in Little Rock, Arkansas, after white people blocked them from entering. That same year, he signed the Civil Rights Act of 1957, a move to protect voter rights by opening the door to federally prosecute anyone who tried to stop someone from voting.

Casting ballots remained a distant concept for some, despite the legislation. Newspapers listed the polling locations and names of each resident in Browns and Uniontown, including Israel Page and Margaret Page. That being said, politics and laws on a statewide level that affected the well-being of Negroes swirled along without much of their input. Granddaddy kept up with the happenings of the time by listening to his radio as the news and the songs permeated his world.

He heard about lynchings, cross burnings, and beatings. He may have even seen such things a time or two. He developed a way of thinking that convinced him everything would be all right—as long as he didn't cause trouble. That's how he got that reputation for being a "good Negro," as they called him. Good Negroes, so to speak, had a better chance of sidestepping the violence others endured.

With all that going on in the backdrop, Fitts finally secured a date for trial: Friday, January 16, 1959. From the neighbors up the road, to the church members, to the men hanging around the Sundown—they all knew Granddaddy would win. How could he not? A man who T-bones another man's car, leaving it totaled and the man's arm disabled, has got to pay. Fitts likely expected that big payout too. Granddaddy sure needed it.

Now, with the anticipation of overdue justice settled in his spirit, Granddaddy unwittingly confirmed what those white men at the door hoped the day before trial. Yes, he told them, if they were looking for Israel "Preacher" Page, they'd found him. They'd searched all over, driving down backcountry roads, they said, because they heard he was a pastor among Negroes. They asked him about the Lord's house. *What are some other churches in the area?* From the stories Granddaddy told, we know that's about how the conversation began anyway, and at some point, they talked like friends in the Lord. With the chill in the air, Granddaddy told them about the sanctuaries nearby. They then went on talking about hunting and dogs, which any country Negro knew a lot about. They hunted for meat, and Granddaddy had a few good beagles. He and Howard turned them loose and followed their lead through the woods, sniffing the scent of easy prey, rabbits and coons. Then Big Mama chopped it up and served it. These so-called ministers knew the routine, since one of them claimed to have a beagle, too, over there in the car. Granddaddy being so knowledgeable about hunting, maybe he could take a look, give them some tips?

When I first read the story years ago of how this kidnapping ploy went down, I didn't understand how it could have occurred so easily. Today I do. Strange white men knocking on the door less than twenty-four hours before the trial might be too suspicious for Big Mama or Dave or maybe even Frank to go along with and hold a conversation. Granddaddy, on the other hand, had white friends in the Radfords and a reputation among whites as a mild-mannered well driller. He experienced racism just like every other Negro, yet he also tasted kindness and cordiality that transcended skin color, at least that's how it must've seemed at the time. Take that mindset and overlay it with two men identifying themselves as ministers, brothers in the Lord. Two *white* men, yes, but in Granddaddy's view, two *friendly* men who talked and even asked for his help with their dog. Men who respected his knowledge, just like the Radfords and the workers on Granddaddy's well-drilling team. No doubt Granddaddy smiled back at them and offered a typical greeting, never suspecting it to be a sham. He tipped his hat and said, "Boss?" That's how I imagine it, since that's who he was.

Granddaddy followed them toward the road, away from the house and just beyond earshot of Big Mama inside. When they reached that car, that's when evil showed itself. The men weren't looking for the Lord's house. No yearning for worship abided in their hearts. And all that chumming about hounds and hunting turned dark. No dog barked from the back seat. Suddenly, they forced Granddaddy inside that car, their expressions turning mean, raw. *Get on in there, nigger.* He asked where they were going, and the barrel of a gun cracked his temple. One man pressed his head down, his cheek hugging the floorboards. There were four men now, two having waited in or near the car while the other two lured him there. They contorted his body to keep his face and gaze down. Passing drivers didn't see Granddaddy in the car, and Granddaddy couldn't get a good look at the other two men in the car.

When it comes to what happened next, relatives' accounts vary slightly, with one sibling remembering something that another didn't mention or couldn't recall. Like tellers of the Gospels, each narrator focused on the scenes that struck meaning in their own hearts. One uncle recalled that the men made a quick stop to drop off one of the four accomplices. Driving slowed, and the tires rumbled against the Alabama earth. But even with his head down, Granddaddy charted their course, the roads running like arteries through his mind. He had grown up here, picked cotton and peanuts on former plantations, climbed trees and run barefoot through fields from Browns to Uniontown. He knew the car had steered to the end of the dirt roadway, turned and squared up with Highway 80—the very road where, more than four years earlier, this whole mess began. He could tell where the engine slowed and paused, pulling up to a farm off the highway. One of the men got out and bid his coconspirators farewell. Granddaddy recognized the voice, not one that he'd heard often but one that he *had* heard and not forgotten.

The car pulled off, and as darkness set in, the miles stretched to places beyond Browns and Uniontown, and Granddaddy lost track of his surroundings. After the car stopped a second time, they forced him out. They guided him deep into a wooded area, as he noted the bridge and body of water mellowing nearby. A night of torment took shape in those woods. The kidnappers wrestled Granddaddy to the ground with their hands and fists, while a garden hose played the main weapon of choice.

"You better drop that case," one of them said.

They kept hitting him, slapping him with that hose—until something happened, something supernatural, as Granddaddy said later in his retellings of the scene. There came a sudden rumbling of the ground, a quaking of sorts. Everything stopped. Except this tremor. Those men looked around the pitch darkness, eyes round with wonder, trying to make out what caused the sound and the shaking. Nothing made sense. Whatever the source, it put the fear of God in those fake preachers, and they "took off running," the only reason they didn't beat Granddaddy closer to death.

By now, his disappearance had the family good and worried. Willie James, Robert Lee, and a friend of the family had returned from their picture show uptown. Around that time, they might have seen anything from *The Blob* to *The Return of Dracula* to a western called *The Badlanders*. Big Mama told them their father had just vanished. Now, a driver could hit the highway within minutes of leaving the house. If Granddaddy just left and the boys were driving in, they figured they might have passed the car with those white men on Highway 80. No one had seen Granddaddy inside because the kidnappers had pressed his head down.

"We knew the trial was coming up," Willie James says. They hoped he'd come walking up the road. They prayed for the positive. Maybe he went to show those men around town. Soon he'd reappear at the front door, ready to wash up and get everything set for court in the morning. Maybe . . .

They asked neighbors and found out theirs wasn't the first house where the white men had stopped. They'd actually gotten lost and stopped by a distant relative's land for directions to Israel Page's house. They wanted to talk to him about churches, at least that's what they said, according to the relative. Not knowing any better, he'd guided the men straight to the Page home.

Night fell, and no streetlights brightened the way in country Alabama, especially around the woods that fenced in rural homes. After the lights dimmed, they couldn't do much searching, and Granddaddy didn't magically reappear as they'd hoped. Nobody slept that night. The later it got, Willie James says, "We knew what had happened then."

Even the little ones tasted anxiety. My mother was away, staying with an elderly relative who needed help. But a granddaughter who'd been in the house at the time says she felt a sense of dread, although she was barely a toddler at the time. She recalls Big Mama walking through the door upset, saying something like, "They got Preacher." "It was very traumatic," she says. "One minute your father is there; then the next, he's gone."

Big Mama did not give up. As soon as the rooster crowed, she got a neighbor to walk the woods and the pasture with her. At some point, she contacted the Uniontown Police Department, which turned the case over to Dallas County, since Browns technically sat outside city limits, within the county's scope of protection. The boys went looking, too. They walked up and down the roads, all around the woods. The cold forced them to take breaks, going back to the house to stand by the fireplace awhile. Then they'd go someplace else. Every place they went in vain only magnified a new reality for them all: They got Daddy.

—⚏—

CHAPTER THIRTEEN

THE KLAN AND ME

I LOOKED STRAIGHT INTO the face of a Klan leader and actually talked to him cordially. Not because I wanted to, not at all. I had been a reporter for the *St. Petersburg Times* in Florida for less than a year when the Ku Klux Klan announced a rally in downtown St. Petersburg. It occurred on a Saturday, which proved most unfortunate for me. I worked the weekend "cops beat," covering crime from the newspaper's main office. On Saturdays, the paper scheduled one daytime cops reporter and one editor per county.

The editor in Pinellas County that morning assigned the story without much expression, saying something like, "The KKK is having a rally downtown." As matter-of-fact as usual, he offered some information about the time and location, then turned back to his computer screen. With no other reporter on duty, the story automatically fell to me.

I stood there, staring at his profile. Did he not see that I am Black? Did he not know that the Klan was a terrorist group known for beating and lynching Black people? But, of course, he knew. He, too, was African American.

Two in a handful of Black journalists working in the paper's newsroom at the time, Sebastian Dortch and I forged a bond during our Saturday shift together. In time, I would spend Thanksgiving with his family, coveting his wife's recipe for sweet potato casserole. We would occasionally do lunch, often talking about faith and family as much as we did stories and newsroom politics.

"KKK rally?" I said, my tone incredulous. Read: *Man, please, are you serious?*

He was. We had to cover the rally in case major protests or news erupted—a possibility since the city had been engulfed in riots sometime before, and racial tensions remained high. The riots started one day in October 1996, after two white police officers stopped Tyron Lewis, an eighteen-year-old Black man, for speeding. The car he drove had been reported stolen, although it was unclear if officers knew that at the time of the stop. (It would be revealed later that an addict sold Lewis the car in exchange for crack cocaine, then reported it stolen.) Officer Jim Knight commanded Lewis to exit the vehicle, but he did not. Instead, Lewis eased the car forward so that the bumper nudged Knight who stood in front of the car. A series of commands and responses followed, ending when Knight shot Lewis through the windshield three times. Lewis died at the scene. Riots ensued over the next few days and again weeks later when a grand jury failed to indict Knight.

Reporters stationed in the newspaper's main office covered ongoing developments in the story. Tuesday through Friday, I worked with a small crew from a satellite office in Clearwater at the time, writing about small-town government issues, human interest stories, and crime on the county's north side. But on Saturdays, when I reported to the main office in St. Petersburg, crumbs from the Lewis killing occasionally fell into my lap. I found bits of news through the National People's Democratic Uhuru Movement, a longtime Black activist group with members who wore daishikis and went by native African names. The word *uhuru* is Swahili for "freedom," and the group led protests against the local police department and called for racial justice.

I worked up my courage when approaching group members, realizing that we shared skin tone and the Black experience in America but differed in our ideological approaches to success. They seemed contently marginalized from the mainstream, decrying injustice from the outside. I, on the other hand, had spent a lifetime making a place for myself within that mainstream, striving to diversify it and create equality from the inside. In the end, we all wanted fair treatment, for our human value to be recognized. Still, the mix of viewpoints could get messy, with one side deeming the other to be either a sellout or too radical. Eventually, I developed a dialogue with an Uhuru about my age. He became my go-to for a quote, to verify information, or to add context to stories that I wrote or information I fed to other reporters.

Over the next quarter century, riots and protests with similar scenarios played out across America. Their inciting incidents involved different people, circumstances, and levels of culpability. And, for me, each case should be taken on its own merits. But they did share the common ingredients of Black men and women dying, perceptions of injustice, and the simmering question of how much America valued life wrapped in black or brown skin. Like tiles on a Scrabble board, letters on protest signs rearranged to spell out Tyron Lewis, then Trayvon Martin, Freddie Gray, Philando Castile, and George Floyd. Differing groups emerged prominently in various cities during any given era to hold white officials accountable: the Nation of Islam, the Black Panther Party, the Uhurus, the Black Lives Matter movement, and other loose networks of protesters.

I watched these uprisings unfold, on an almost rhythmic timeline. I'd stare at the TV screen or computer monitor, listening to commentators in the twenty-four-hour news cycle, watching videos of family members and protesters entrenched in whichever city the action took place. Then, in 2020, when Officer Derek Chauvin put his knee on George Floyd's neck for 9 minutes and 29 seconds, killing him and sparking an outcry that reverberated worldwide, finally I moved from in front of the screen to the protest scene. No longer a journalist, my involvement in the news could not be deemed a conflict of interest.

Floyd died nearly six hundred miles away, but protesters in downtown Fort Wayne joined the universal voice that demanded an end to police brutality against people of color. In the midsized midwestern city, some protestors smashed business windows and looted after dark. Police spewed tear gas and rubber bullets. I didn't support any of that. I wanted to be part of a peaceful, organized protest rather than just driving by. One day, I drove downtown for an organized rally that involved public officials, community leaders, and young adults. I stood among them on the courthouse lawn and listened to speakers demand justice. Another day, faith leaders led a march across the Dr. Martin Luther King Jr. Memorial Bridge, and I chanted along with more than a hundred others, saying the same things that African Americans said during the civil rights movement, just a few years after Granddaddy's kidnapping. Sixty years later, "No justice, no peace" remained relevant.

The backdrop now looked much different than the documentaries I saw back then, though. Some days, I saw more white people than people of color. They brought their children along, calling it a teachable moment to participate in justice. They hoisted signs that called out their white counterparts.

Stop disguising racism as nationalism

White silence is violence

One sign I found particularly poignant, given Granddaddy's story: *I will not go silently back to the 1950s.*

Where were these people when the Klan rallied one Saturday on my cops shift years earlier, the day I had to cover the men in starched white robes? I wished they'd been there, or even a string of Uhurus in headwraps from the motherland. But none of them showed up. Just a smattering of costumed men walking single file down the street, toting ominous signs. Everyday people, most of them white, passed in a hurry, distancing themselves, making their way to or from whatever shop or parked car awaited.

Details blur today, but I recall stopping a few passers-by, scribbling their reactions to the men marching and holding white supremacist signs in late-1990s

America. Most did not want to comment on the record. If reporters from other news outlets showed up, I didn't notice them. Downtown St. Petersburg would wait another few years to be reinvented with a stream of new businesses, restaurants, and waterfront hotels. But nothing really drew a crowd when the rally occurred, not even the Klan. I made for a pitiful audience, standing on the other side of the street, jotting scenic notes. The sun beaming down. The Klan signs saying whatever they said. The costumes with pointy-tip hoods that opened in front, so you could see the person's face.

I didn't want to talk to the Klansmen or even get within arm's length. I disdained them, yes, but another feeling drove my hesitation even more, one that I tried to ignore: fear. Thoughts of Granddaddy's kidnapping didn't flood my mind at the time. I did not mentally float to 1950s Browns, Alabama. I just felt scared. Of what, I couldn't exactly articulate. We stood out in the open air, in the middle of the day, in full view of presumably sane, nonracist people walking by. Yet I trembled at the thought of getting close to those men. I wanted to turn away, go back to the newsroom, report on a festival or car crash or anything else. But duty demanded I complete my assignment, which meant doing what I'd been putting off since I arrived. I had to talk to the Klan, get their side of the story, no matter how ridiculous that other side seemed. First, I exhausted all the adjectives I could record in my notepad about the weather and colors and location. Now, with time stretching on, I just had to do it. I straightened my back, crossed the street, and walked toward the guy at the front of the Klan line.

Picture it, a twenty-three-year-old African American woman standing in front of a white man in full Klan regalia. She holds a skinny reporter's notepad in her left hand and a pen in her right. His face, at least the part she can see, looks older than middle-age with graying eyebrows, but she decides beforehand not to call him "sir." No, attempting to preserve a morsel of dignity, she refuses to use her typical pleasantries. In retrospect, she could have processed this moment differently. She could have felt empowered that these clowns could no longer stop her from achieving her dream of becoming a writer. She could have marched over there, stood confidently in their faces, and looked them in the eye—something Granddaddy and his ancestors seldom did. She could have seen herself as an example of how the plan for white supremacy had steadily crumbled. But in the moment, her perspective is skewed. Instead of feeling empowered, she feels weak, demoralized, considering that she owes the white supremacist her professionalism, at least enough to offer an interview, a platform to voice his foolishness.

She intentionally looks him square in the eyes at first. "Excuse me," she says simply. She tries to sound strong voiced, but confidence breaks down, and fear creeps in as nervousness. Her voice shakes a little when she asks for his name. He notices and smirks, as if this shakiness satisfies him. He spells his name, and she writes it quickly, then asks a question so insignificant it can't be called to mind now. She walks away, hoping that her back is straight with some semblance of courage on the outside. On the inside, humiliation simmers. She determines that a portion of her is still bound somehow. Where is the freedom, the essence of uhuru in her? And would she ever find it? She would not speak about this piece of the memory, the actual encounter, holding it at a distance for years to come.

On the short drive back to the office, I focused on constructing the story in my head. My notebook held only a few quotes and notes about the sun, a breeze, and a low turnout—quite "thin" on actual news as journalists would say. I would keep it short, paint a picture, and segue into brief remarks from the Klan guy and passers-by, presenting both sides as objectively as the granddaughter of Israel Page could. I walked through the building lobby, went up the elevator, and strode across the newsroom to the editor's desk to summarize my notes.

"*So nobody came?*" he said.

"*Not really,*" I told him.

"*Nothing happened?*"

"*Nope,*" I said.

"*Never mind. We won't write anything about it.*"

I stared at him again. Part of me wanted to say, *After all I went through?* Another part exhaled in relief because I didn't have to concoct a story out of this. Years later, I called Sebastian to talk through this experience with him. We'd kept in contact after I left the paper, yet I never mentioned this assignment. He didn't remember any of it but agreed that my version of events seemed likely. He started working at the paper a short time before the Tyron Lewis protests began, so the riots and lingering racial tensions helped frame what might be counted as news. He understood that the assignment was awkward for me, but as journalists we couldn't avoid certain stories based on our skin color, no more than a white journalist could.

"This was a story," he said, and we were not going to allow these "knuckleheads [the Klan] to stop us from covering it."

He took it a step further. From his view, it would have been an insult to my skills as a journalist *not* to expect me to complete the assignment. He added, "I think that would have been degrading."

CHAPTER FOURTEEN

—⚏—

FAITH VS. FEAR

GRANDDADDY SPENT the night lying in the cold woods, after divine intervention rumbled like a quake and scared those men off. He awoke from a deep sleep, or likely unconsciousness, and lumbered about, trying to figure his surroundings and get his thoughts together. One family account has him hearing the men come back for him, apparently after the rumbling ceased. Now they wanted to kill him for sure, but he hid and stayed quiet. This time they left for good, and he stayed awake and as alert as he could. By dawn, the brightening sky lit up the terrain.

He later would tell a newspaper reporter, "When the sun come up, I got my bearings and started walking south."

He knocked on the door of a home where a Negro family lived and asked the location. Highway 14, they told him. He knew 14 ran into Highway 80, which could take him in the direction of home. With bruises on his skin and blood staining his clothes, he trudged along the highway for a short while before realizing he had another option. An all-too-familiar homestead stood nearby. He made his way there, approached, and knocked. His old friend Cecil Radford stood on the other side of the door.

Radford listened to Granddaddy's story and offered to help however he could. Soon they sat in Radford's car, heading down Highway 80 toward Browns. Granddaddy didn't have him go all the way home but rather to the Sundown Ranch, perhaps hoping to get a friend there to take him the rest of the way. They arrived around one o'clock, and it just so happened that Willie James and Robert Lee had gone there in the continued search for their father. They were telling some of the regulars what had happened when Preacher Page himself stumbled in. Everybody in the place stared, as if they'd seen a ghost, taking in the fact that the kidnapping victim now stood before their eyes.

"He started crying and said he was glad to see us," Robert Lee said. "Well, I was crying, too, 'cause we had been up all night."

Then they stepped back and got a good look at him.

"He was bleeding," Robert Lee said.

"When he got in, he came in with bruises all over him," says Willie James. "I did lose it. I started crying. I just turned and walked outside. I didn't want to look at him."

Granddaddy had Cecil Radford drive him to the Sundown Ranch because he didn't initially want to go back to the house, Robert Lee said. Perhaps he wanted to stay away because of his appearance. Still, he had to go home sooner or later, and, I suspect, his sons' presence eased his tension a little. They all stayed at the Sundown a while. Cecil Radford eventually left and went on his way, although the scene didn't leave his mind or his heart, his son would tell me years later.

Commotion had spread from the family house to the police department to the courthouse in Selma. When Granddaddy didn't show up for trial, court officials organized a search. When he showed up later that day, a chief deputy with the Dallas County Sheriff's Office and the game warden launched an investigation into his kidnapping and beating. Circuit Solicitor Blanchard McLeod later joined them in a visit to the Page home, where McLeod recorded Granddaddy's sequence of events, including quotes of his version of the story.

The next day, the *Selma Times-Journal* reporter Arthur Capell, who would go on to report much of the civil rights developments in Alabama, found Granddaddy at the Sundown Ranch again, likely after going to the house and asking where he might be. Capell asked for an interview, taking notes, scribbling quotes and reactions, to complement the circuit solicitor's report, as well as court records that detailed the original traffic accident in 1954.

"I'm going to church tomorrow and ask for the Lord's guidance," Granddaddy told him. He told Capell that he'd never seen his attackers before and couldn't identify them, but the family knew better. At least three of the attackers may have been outsiders from Talladega County or friends of the deputy in the original accident. But Granddaddy could identify the fourth. From various accounts, it's unclear whether the fourth attacker joined in the beating or just involved himself in the kidnapping, before being dropped off at his farm. Those men needed someone local to guide them through twisting back roads in search of Preacher Page's place. Even with the fourth man in the car, they still got lost and had to stop and ask for directions. But Granddaddy left out that detail, that someone from his hometown had participated. After all that had happened and the threats during the beating, he feared the consequences. The article quoted Granddaddy by using stereotypical phonetic spellings, as reporters often did when it came to southern Blacks—although they did not do the same for southern whites, who rarely used perfect diction themselves.

"It's got bigger than me now, Boss," Granddaddy told the reporter. "I just don't know what course to take. I just ain't able to get myself together a bit. . . . I'm afraid for myself and my family—I've got eight chillun [sic] at my house, Boss."

Granddaddy went on to say he only sought his just due. "But then on the other hand, it don't seem like what I'm doing is wrong, since that wreck done hindered me from carrying on in the business I was brought up in and followed for nigh onto 30 years. It troubles a man inside when he ain't stout enough to do what he believes."

The story went on:

> "Preacher Page," defended by white people in the Browns community as a "good Negro," worked as a well digger for Cecil Radford "and for his papa, Mr. O.B. Radford before him," for almost 30 years before the July 1954 wreck, which cost him the use of his right arm.
>
> Since that time he has been physically unable to dig wells and has "farmed as best I could using my chillun, and done a little preaching."
>
> "I can manage a hoe sorta' halfway by resting it agin' [sic] my leg and chopping left handed," he said with gestures of explanation. "But I can't do no plowing a' tall. I just can't hold no plow stock and manage no mule with one hand."

The article continued,

> The Negro hasn't dug a well since the mishap:
> "But I wish I could, boss," he said yesterday with the enthusiasm of hungering for the task. "Cold as it is I'd be out there putting a hole in the ground right now, if I could."

Officials delayed the trial after learning about the kidnapping. The Dallas County Sheriff's Office offered police protection until the case could be rescheduled, so a judge could hear Granddaddy's original complaint about the car accident. But Granddaddy wasn't convinced they could—*would*—keep him and his family safe. Should he continue with the trial or just drop the whole thing? He saw pros and cons either way, according to the *Selma Times-Journal*.

"It's just near 'bout five of this and five of that, ain't it, Boss?"

"I could go up there to the jail and be safe myself until the hearing, if it's ever heard. But then what about my family whilst I'm away? And what about after the trial is over? The police can keep watch over me for a while, but they can't keep no guard on me from now on."

"I just don't know where my feeling is at now and I gotta pray over it awhile," he said. The Negro added: "I got a puppy out there at my house and hit's jest his nature to carry on an bark, particular at night. And ever time he barks, I jump. I believe I'se nigh onto a nervous breakdown."

He wouldn't move forward with the trial any time soon, Granddaddy said. He needed time to calm his nerves. "I don't feel like I'd be able to testify, I'm so tore up," he said. "I doubts I could tell exactly what happened in the wreck now and say just how everything happened."

According to Capell, "Page was reluctant to speculate on why he was beaten and mentioned only once, and then briefly that 'they said I'd better drop the case, or something like that.'"

The story continued: "But the frightened Negro, whose fierce pride allowed him to use the word 'scairt' only once, did say: 'I've been studying over it and I just can't account for no other reason anyone would want to whip me. I didn't know I was doing nothing contrary.... I've been here 50 years, Boss. I growed up here, and I ain't never had no trouble with nobody before.'"

Granddaddy explained his reasons for resorting to a lawsuit: "I couldn't do no work, $498 worth of doctor's bills had piled up," he said, referring to initial bills rather than the ultimate total. "I had been called in about the case two or three times without nothing being done, so I went to see Mr. Fitts and turned it over to him."

Granddaddy told Capell how he roused from unconsciousness before daylight and wandered to the road but had to stop till the sun came up because he didn't know where he was.

"When the sun come up, I got my bearings and started walking south," he said.

Capell told the rest of the story about Granddaddy's final journey back home and that law enforcement started an investigation into the kidnapping. According to Capell, the solicitor, McLeod, "described Page as being 'severely beaten' about the body and head but said he was unmarked, except for a slight cut on his face left by the pistol lick, because a rubber hose was used."

The backlash for beating a well-liked Negro like Granddaddy came swiftly and, perhaps, from surprising sources, given the era. Even local attorneys formally condemned the kidnapping and beating, adopting an official resolution to reflect their feelings:

Be it resolved that the Dallas County Bar Association deplores and con-
demns the recent treatment of Israel Page by persons unknown, and respect-
fully urges the law enforcement officers of Dallas County to thoroughly
investigate the case, and if possible, apprehend and bring the parties before
the courts of Dallas County where justice can be done.

Be it further resolved, in the event of any litigation in Dallas County by
any persons whomsoever, that the Bar is opposed to and against any intimi-
dation of said litigant, either by words, physical violence, threats, damage
to his property or any other method which would intimidate said litigant in
pursuing his grievance in the Courts of Dallas County, Alabama, in cases of
similar nature.

Court officials rescheduled the case for January 22. Fitts reissued subpoenas
for his witnesses: Dr. George B. Nicholson, who had treated Granddaddy at
Vaughan Memorial Hospital; Johnnie Walter, a friend of the family who lived
near Marion Junction; W. T. Buck, who sold that old Chevy to Granddaddy in
the first place; and W. H. Rainey, with the State Highway Department, where
the accident report rested in file.

Granddaddy would have to show up, too. He would have to swear to tell the
truth and state his version of the events as they took place on July 15, 1954. He
had to overcome the fear of those white men following through on the threats
they'd made in the woods and to trust that if he told the truth, if he kept pushing for justice, everything would be all right.

But sometimes it's hard to know which way to go with God, even for a
preacher. Should he believe God would protect the family if he went forward
with the case and just keep pushing ahead? Or, perhaps, God's will didn't mean
justice in the courtroom this time. Maybe God wanted Granddaddy to let the
whole thing go and have faith that he would provide for the family somehow,
despite their financial tragedy.

Before the kidnapping, Granddaddy felt sure of his success in the courtroom. He believed God would grant victory against Brantley Lee and the rest
of the Talladega establishment. But now came so many questions. It would be
cruel to label his thoughts as doubting God. Human nature leads us to pause
at a time like this, to think—really think—about what to do next. Granddaddy
kept weighing this side and that, while the people around him set their minds
on retribution. Robert Radford couldn't recite the long-ago details, but he recalled his father felt "hurt" because some men had beaten Granddaddy. He
wanted to know who orchestrated the attack.

"My father went and tried to find the people who beat him," Robert Radford said. "He would've beat the hell out of them."

The Bible says vengeance is the Lord's, but others wanted a piece of the assailants, too. The family kept the news from Frank, but they couldn't stop it from reaching Granddaddy's oldest son, who lived in Brooksville, Florida, by this time. When word of the kidnapping reached Dave Page, he behaved true to character. He and Howard, who also lived in Brooksville at the time, made the nine-hour journey home. Dave burst through the front door, chest poked out and mad as a hedgehog with fire in his lungs.

"Who was it, Daddy?" he demanded, ready to handle his business. "Who was it?"

Despite Granddaddy's sketchy account to the solicitor general and newspaper reporter of being unable to identify anyone, Negroes in town knew better. Preacher Page had drilled wells for houses all over the area for decades, so people knew he could identify the white men in Browns and Uniontown. And even if the kidnappers were outsiders, they couldn't snake their way through those back roads without a guide.

Now Dave figured he needed to show those white men what backcountry justice looked like, what it felt like. He wanted to get his hands on at least one of the cowards. He wanted to look that cracker in the eye, let him know Dave Page wasn't scared of his pale skin, not one bit. If Frank Page was *that*, then Dave, three years older, was the original *that*. Granddaddy sensed his son had every intention of making good on his threats and knew better than to answer Dave's question.

"He wouldn't tell us who did it," Howard said. "Because if he had told Dave, he would've gave him hell."

Dave's determination for payback actually did the opposite of what he intended. Granddaddy held the man's identity even closer, at least for a while. He told no one. The case grew bigger than him now—that's what he told the reporter, and he meant it. The attackers may have been KKK "brothers," so to speak. Plenty of Klansmen lived in the area, although Negroes didn't know their identities. Like Frank said, they donned their costumes and rode on horseback down Nigger Street to shoo Negroes back home at night. Granddaddy figured one Negro, even a fearless, pigheaded one, could not overtake them. He couldn't let his son get killed or spur retaliation against the whole family, trying to get back at one white man.

Still, plenty of friends and relatives urged Granddaddy to go forward with the original traffic case. He shouldn't let those men stop him from getting the settlement that belonged to him. To win, he just had to get on the stand and officially give his version of the accident. One relative, called Uncle Rich, visited and almost begged him to follow through.

"Too much money to let it all go—and you deserve to have it," he told Granddaddy.

Everybody knew the family struggled to make a living and pay off all those hospital bills since the accident. Perhaps as a motivator, one relative gave Granddaddy a warning: If he didn't make a move and get on that stand, he'd better not come asking for financial help. They had their own families to take care of and couldn't help Granddaddy when Granddaddy refused to speak up for himself.

Willie James remembered the tension coming down on Granddaddy from every side. He wanted his father to testify, too, but he sympathized with his position. "I understood the fear that was in him," Willie James says. "I told him, as bad as I wanted that money, and I wanted it bad, but I didn't have no anger or no ill feelings of him not wanting to get on that stand."

Big Mama, meanwhile, leaned on her faith as she always had. Whatever Granddaddy's decision—settlement or no settlement—she knew the Lord would make a way for the Pages to come through. While Granddaddy wavered back and forth, God only knows what Big Mama whispered in his ear. She would keep right on humming and singing on that front pew at church, whatever her husband decided. She would help her family survive and, somehow, feel they were tasting a bit of God's glory along the way. This world is a mean world, that much she knew, and not even a winning court case would change that.

Various factors played into the final decision, as best we can tell. One of them, perhaps among the strongest, came from a visit with Mr. Coleman Long, a respected businessman who owned the land where the family had lived since they'd left Buck's property. Long came driving up the road some time after the kidnapping, and his presence put everyone on alert. It was no mystery why he had come. The kidnapping hovered in Browns, Uniontown, and Selma, where the lawyers voted on their resolution for diligence in making an arrest, and Granddaddy's story continued to spread.

Willie James, and likely the rest of the family, too, hoped Long and other whites would stand up for his father against the attackers. If Granddaddy moved forward with the lawsuit, they needed more than big talk and revenge. They needed more than promises of protection from police. Law enforcement could only do so much—and sometimes they lurked behind the corruption themselves. That much rang true, since Brantley Lee himself wore a badge for many years but now evaded civil law. Long, a prominent Democrat, property owner, and Uniontown businessman, could give the boost they all needed to pursue justice without fear.

Long sat down in a modest area that served as both sitting room and bed-room. All the while, Willie James stood nearby, listening, hoping for a break-through, some way that this tragedy could turn around again in the family's favor. He listened, and I'm sure Long expressed his sorrow over the whole thing. But only this part stuck out for Willie James: Long kept explaining why the family should let it go. Regrettably, Long said, some people involved might be high-ranking. Back in those days, it was hard to know who belonged to the Klan or who just saw nothing wrong with conspiring against Negroes. Long said local law enforcement or business owners or politicians might be involved somehow. This thing would get messy, too messy, if Granddaddy kept it going.

I imagine Long chose his words carefully. Willie James summarizes them like this: "Now, we *could* find out who did it, but we're not."

Granddaddy took it in. Long's perspective claimed the pursuit of justice for Granddaddy would cause more harm than good. Today, it's hard to judge what Long felt inside or how he weighed the circumstances. He'd fought in World War I and held a reputation for being fair to the local Negroes. In the end, Granddaddy bid him farewell and digested this new reality. Long and likely many others Granddaddy had talked with uptown would not become the strong allies he hoped for, not now.

The dynamic crushed Willie James, just shy of twenty years old back then.

"I saw at that time that a man was not a man"—at least not in the South, he told me a half century later. Growing up, Willie James knew whites deemed Negroes as less than. Still, hearing the conversation with Mr. Long only deep-ened his doubts about the hearts of white people, even the so-called good ones.

"They didn't care about us," he explains. "They beat a man up. He can't take care of his family, and they don't want to expose the person who did it—be-cause it might be somebody important?"

Frustrations that had built up inside Willie James over the past four years bubbled over. The audacity, the cruelty of the events, replayed in his mind. The big-time whites, the ones who called his father a "good Negro"—they couldn't do anything about this. No, they *wouldn't* do anything about it. Willie James had lived his whole life running up and down country roads, soaking in an atmosphere that called him inferior to white men whose power lay in pushing another man down. That had to end, he told Granddaddy.

"I'm going up north," he declared later. "I want to go where a man is treated like a man."

Granddaddy looked at him, likely with a little less hope in his eyes than he had before, certainly since he'd filed the lawsuit certain of victory. He responded in his calm, slow drawl, as he spoke to Willie James words my uncle would forever remember:

"Son," Granddaddy told him, "you gon' be just as black when you cross that Mason-Dixon line as you is now."

—ɯ—

TURNING MESS INTO MINISTRY

WE DON'T TARRY LONG at this juncture of the story. No sense in dwelling in the disappointment of Granddaddy dropping the biggest case of his life and for some of his children, the biggest of their lives, too. The good thing is, after a while, Granddaddy shifted his perspective on the matter from disappointment to hope, as only a preacher could. Despair is a jagged rock to land on in any situation, and he refused to let this story stay there. He retreated instead to another rock, one where he'd found solace in the past, since the day his calling stirred, and Big Mama told him to go on and answer. This rock, as one old spiritual put it, is the "rock in a weary land," better known as Jesus.

A different man might have set his faith aside, pushed the mourning bench out of his mind, questioned why God allowed such suffering. Granddaddy did not. He couldn't. Faith had embedded herself in his soul since the days he preached to a sanctuary of corn stalks and cotton bolls, likely long before his little brother Frank and their siblings played his congregation.

And so, sometime after *Israel Page v. Brantley Lee* fell silent in Browns and Uniontown, after the courthouse clerk filed it away for the next forty-six years, when Granddaddy got his strength back and he'd settled in his mind what the Lord would want him to do next—one Sunday morning after all this, the Rev. Page set aside his street clothes and put on his Sunday suit. He topped it off with a brimmed hat and cranked up the replacement Chevy his son Howard had bought, then steered with his good left hand along those red dirt roads. He stopped at the church house, where he and Big Mama stepped inside a familiar sanctuary. She sat up front, and whichever children hadn't already grown up and moved out took their seats.

No piano or drums, the music played out in handclaps, foot stomps, and hymns, some handed down from slaves who held tight to faith while working in fields. Soon someone would strike a note, whatever song was on his heart that day, and everybody else joined in, singing and sometimes moaning. Big Mama often led the worship. "I'm on the battlefield," she'd sing, "working for my Lord." No doubt, uncertainty simmered just beneath the melody, with folks anticipating what Preacher Page would say to the people he led after enduring what some would call defeat.

No one remembers Granddaddy's words on his return to the pulpit, but we all know a seasoned preacher can turn just about any hardship into a blessing, depending on how he delivers the message and the passion behind it. For years to come, Granddaddy used the pulpit to tell the story of his kidnapping—in a way that had the people praising God, no less. And I can hear his sermonic version, mingled with shouts of joy and response from the people.

The men came to his house, tricked him, forced him into the car, Granddaddy would say. They put his face to the floorboards; then they drove and drove and drove, till they came to a wooded area miles away from home. They beat him with that rubber hose. Thought it would do him in, but it didn't. They threatened him. They tried—oh, how they tried—to kill him in the woods that night. But God wouldn't let it be so.

Amen, Preacher!

Next thing you know, "the earth shook like a drunken man." That's what Granddaddy liked to say about that night, paraphrasing Isaiah 24:20. The ground started rocking and a-reeling, reeling and a-rocking. Those kidnappers got so scared they didn't know what to do, and they ran off. See, the devil wanted to kill Preacher Page that night, but God wouldn't let it be so.

Glory to his name!

Granddaddy told the story over and over again, so much so that Big Mama tired of hearing it. "You need to stop talking about it so much," she'd tell him. But Granddaddy did not stop. Behind the pulpit, in a rocking chair on the porch with neighbors—or really wherever the occasion lent itself to a retelling—he spoke of a God who spared his life, saved him from the brood of evil that came to snuff him out one cool January evening. In Granddaddy's version, the names of Brantley Lee, his attorney, the Talladega County commissioners who did nothing, and the local accomplice fade. Their identities prove of little importance. They are the devil's puppets, stand-ins for a racist system, pawns used to carry out a plot much bigger than one court case. The real battle is a spiritual one, with good and evil wrestling over the Black man's faith, faith that remained steadfast through slavery, Jim Crow, the Tuskegee experiment, eugenics, police brutality, and every other dart of injustice.

Still, this story and its complementary sermon couldn't delete the pain and trauma that simmered down deep, preventing some from fully embracing his testimony of victory in the Lord. Granddaddy may not have seen himself as fully victorious. I believe the trauma quietly followed him on strolls along the road, on drives uptown, when he pulled a sleeve over his lame arm in the morning time, all of it dogging him in ways he could not express. I myself struggled, asking more than once, "Why am I writing this?" I dug deep through archives and family accounts to unearth evidence of triumph, in the sense that people today think of winning. I found a good-natured man who praised God for sparing his life, although that same God did not balance the scales of justice for him or for African Americans still struggling for equity today.

I settled on the matter where I suspect Granddaddy decided to. We all experience tragedy in some form, no matter our skin color or wealth or lack of it. Even the Bible says we should consider life's trials with joy *when*—not *if*—we face them. "Consider it pure joy, my brothers and sisters, whenever you face trials of many kinds, because you know that the testing of your faith produces perseverance." One thing Granddaddy proved: he knew how to persevere. If evil had its way, Preacher Page would've been gone in 1959, his body buried six feet under, his soul prematurely resting with God. The next best thing, from evil's perch, would've been for him to live but lose his faith, diminish all hope. Neither happened. The attackers did get him, but they couldn't hold him for good, not physically or spiritually. To the contrary, Granddaddy did what any good preacher would do. He turned one of the most tragic events of his life into a sermon, or, as a common saying in the Black church goes, he turned his mess into his ministry.

Everybody had their own mess to deal with in life, but come Sunday, Granddaddy preached, and people praised God. He'd already set aside time to read and study his Bible, outlining the points of his message, often using a pencil and notebook paper to write out the words and scriptures for church. The handwriting deteriorated after the accident because he had to write with his left hand. In a small collection of his handwritten sermons, I keyed in on one titled "Life's Territory." The notes have him starting with a talk about the Israelites and their Promised Land, or rather their territory. From there he gave a for-instance of how government officials at the time planned to expand the United States' borders by making Alaska a state. In the same way, God wanted to expand our personal borders, Granddaddy said, referring to "life's territory."

I wasn't inside the church back then, but it reads like the part of a sermon that comes just before the climax, when the *amens* sputter across the church and the women wave fans to get some air because suddenly it's a bit warm in here.

"I'm saying there's various territories in this present life, and it's to each of us to possess it," Granddaddy wrote. "We have a broad territory."

Hallelujahs would bounce off the walls by then. People who heard him in his heyday knew Rev. Page could preach. That's one reason Howard followed on his father's heels any chance he could. Howard couldn't help but listen good when Granddaddy stood at the front of the church house and the crowd got to swaying and the spirit got high. Like most Black Baptist preachers then, a handkerchief or other swath of cloth sat nearby to wipe the sweat from his jowls and brow.

"I loved to hear him preach," Uncle Howard told me. "He could just get in that Bible and tell you, and he'd be preaching, and women would be jumping up and shouting and carrying on."

It was Howard that I called during one of my Alabama research trips. I wanted to visit one of Granddaddy's churches. Of those he pastored through the years, relatives knew for sure that El Bethel still stood. I mapped out directions, only to wind up at another church altogether. I didn't use GPS in 2011, so I needed guidance, real guidance, the kind that knows how to maneuver country twists and turns to a little church in Alabama. Howard had tagged along with Granddaddy for well jobs, hunting, and preaching. He would know the way.

We knew Howard as one of several jokesters in the family but also the go-to at family reunions or special dinner events that called for an opening prayer. Howard would step up and take the mic. No saint himself, those church services he attended with Granddaddy still left a mark on him. In keeping with the old Baptist tradition of whooping, he sang his prayers, which really were half heavenly pleas and half storytelling. An Uncle Howard prayer might be described as opera meets the blues *and* the Lord, all at the same time. During one event, his prayer song told the story of having stopped at a traffic light that turned red, then green, while the sun was shining, before he somehow tied it to Jesus hanging on the cross. He struck notes of anguish but also hope, and we had to pay attention with bowed heads to keep up with the mini plots delivered in scratchy melody. Times like these, we appreciated the typical buffet style for our family gatherings, because the food stayed warm atop burners until we could fix our plates.

Yes, even after all these years, Uncle Howard would know the way to the church. Already behind the steering wheel, I called from my cell phone. He asked where I was. Just like Granddaddy, he knew the land, the markers, without seeing them. El Bethel, he said, stood off 80 and Tayloe Road. I kept him on the line and put him on speaker as I looked for a subtle dirt path, a little cut off the highway, as he instructed. I wouldn't be able to see the actual church from the road, he told me, only a slender path.

"Just north of the railroad tracks," he said, "right there between Uniontown and Browns."

Finally, a cut in the scenery. Steering into the curve, I saw the rugged wooden sign that read "El Bethel." I thanked Uncle Howard and parked near a spattering of cars. Inside, the traditional-style sanctuary with its maple-colored wood furnishings, took me back to my childhood in Jerusalem Baptist. At El Bethel, blue carpet covered the flooring beneath, while blue fabric upholstered the pews. A wooden table displayed the words "This do in remembrance of me," and I envisioned suited deacons and assistant pastors gathering around it to dispense Communion, just as we had done in Fort Wayne long ago. Two large flower arrangements bookended the table, not likely fresh in early December. Modest stained-glass windows skewed the dreary weather outside. I spotted a couple of floor heaters, but they weren't turned on, and a chill hung in the air. A large, framed proclamation of some sort, titled "Church Covenant," hung on the wall. The room looked tidy, with only the style of furnishing and some cracks in the white walls betraying the church's age. A portrait of the traditional white American Jesus with long hair hung prominently, watching over the scene.

I'd arrived in the middle of Sunday school, it seemed, and the Rev. Edward Moore was discussing the week's lesson with a handful of his members sitting up front. They turned to see who'd entered, then eyed each other curiously. No one recognized me from the familiar faces around town, but they asked no questions, assuming a visitor decided to join them for the day. Someone motioned for me to come up front. I did, and they proceeded with the lesson.

Rev. Moore stood behind a lectern, putting on his glasses when he needed to read a scripture, then taking them off again. He wore a dark blue double-breasted suit that matched the pews, with a brighter royal blue shirt, a paisley tie, and black shoes. He saved his black pastoral robe for later, when the more formal Sunday service started at 11:30 a.m., but I would have to be on the road for a nine-hour drive back to Florida by then. A deacon and a woman in a red dress affirmed the pastor's remarks from the pulpit with nods and *mm-hmms*.

"Some of the Israelites were so close to the Promised Land, they could look over and see it," he was saying.

"Mm-hmm."

"But they still were not able to cross over," Moore said. "History repeats itself."

"Mm-hmm."

They shouldn't be like those Israelites, falling short of their Promised Land, Moore said. God "put all of us here to do something, and what I like about Jesus is he didn't waste no time doing what he was supposed to do."

I could see Granddaddy up there, standing on the pulpit, talking about a similar theme of life purpose, framing his message around the idea of claiming the territory God has for each of us. After Rev. Moore's lesson, I introduced myself to the small group as Israel Page's granddaughter. Several remembered him and my mother, as well. They asked about family members who'd moved to Fort Wayne and they hadn't seen in a while. Some called Granddaddy the "Rev. I. S. Page," the "I. S." being short for "Israel." People knew him to always wear a brimmed hat, Rev. Moore said.

Rev. Moore had grown up in El Bethel and attended the church when Granddaddy pastored there for a number of years. "He was OK with me," Moore said. Later he would show me a photo of Granddaddy printed along with other El Bethel pastors. The church had compiled the photos and printed them for a history program they'd held in recent years.

Of course, he remembered the kidnapping, he said, because Rev. Page used to talk about it. "Back in those days, white men, they was real low-down," he said. "They took him off and fooled him. . . . He said they had left him for dead and he crawled away."

By 2014, I felt an intimacy with Granddaddy, a connection that gave me enough confidence to tell his story out loud. A speaking assignment for a large church congregation opened the door. Mine would be part of a themed series during the summer months where different speakers each week chose a topic that hinged on a well-known song title. I'd spoken for churches before, but this occasion unnerved me. For the first time, Granddaddy would be there with me in spirit. Not to mention that it was a mixed congregation, but majority white. It felt right, though. I wanted to talk about overcoming adversity and pursuing one's calling. What better example than Granddaddy? I titled it, "Ease on Down the Road," after the popular song from *The Wiz*, using the song's refrain as encouragement to brush off shortcomings, distractions, and wrong turns in life, to get back on track and ease along God's charted path.

I gave examples of other life detours to overcome, and then launched into Granddaddy's story midway through my talk. I told of the accident, the lawyer, and Granddaddy's faith for a victory in the courtroom. I told of the tragic kidnapping, the threats, and the ultimate decision to dismiss the case. Then, I said, "I know some of you are looking at me, and you're like, 'Why is she telling us this story.' Because that wasn't the ending that you expected.

"I tell you that story, not *in spite of* the fact that Preacher lost so much. I tell that story *because* of it. And because I know that many of you have lost, as well. On life's road, you have lost. I have lost. You lost the husband. He left you. You lost the wife. You lost the loved one that you prayed that God would heal. You lost the career. You lost the business that you had invested everything in. You lost. . . . Just like Preacher."

I stood in the spotlight on the darkened stage, in front of a vast crowd that had turned completely silent. I anticipated as much, the topic being too heavy for hand claps. An old photo of Granddaddy flashed on screens behind me. I went on, "Oh, but one day, my Granddaddy got up. Preacher got up. Can you see him?" I said, looking into the distance, seeing him in my mind's eye. "I can envision him, getting up now and taking that left hand and putting on his hat that he always wore. I can see Preacher picking up his Bible now with his left hand. And I can see Preacher easing again on down that red dirt road.

"I can see Preacher. He's headed now to the church house. And people all over now are wondering, 'What you gonna do, Preacher?' And Preacher stood there, and he told them with his actions. Preacher kept on preaching because that was what he was called to do. . . . Oh, everybody was talking about how Preacher had lost the case. But Preacher said, you know what, they left me for dead in the woods. . . . By the grace of God, I made it."

I talked about how my grandfather had heard the story of Jonah being saved from the belly of a whale, but now he knew for himself what it was like to experience the life-saving power of God. With this, Preacher turned his most traumatic detour into a sermon and kept easing down life's road. And Granddaddy's captors never imagined that what started on Highway 80 in the 1950s would travel through generations to Israel Page's granddaughter and live on as a story of overcoming sixty years later.

The good part, I told them, is that just as he walked with Preacher, "God is walking with you on your road. He is not leaving you alone. He's right there with you. Loving on you. Directing you. Guiding you. And he's saying come on, come on, come to know me. Understand my love for you, because when we do that, we make real the scripture in Romans 8 where it says, 'Yet in all these things we are more than conquerors—*more than conquerors*—through Him who loved us.'"

No *amens* or *mm-hmms* rang forth as I spoke, this being a nondenominational crowd with an evangelical bent. Still, plenty of heads nodded in agreement. I gave the message at all four weekend services, and I felt good about the impact, at least for a while. Then the evening set, and there came a call from one of the church's staff leaders, an older white man with whom I'd had plenty of light-hearted and meaningful conversations in the past. After some small talk, he revealed concerns about my message that weekend. My grandfather's story struck some wrong notes in this integrated church. It made him "feel guilty," he said.

White people behaved shamefully all those years ago, he explained. But the white people in this modern church were not the racists of yesteryear. Bringing up the past only sparked discomfort. "And I wasn't the only one who felt that way," he said.

The shock of what he said left me momentarily speechless. The church had already undergone an intentional effort to diversify. Church leaders called meetings with members of color to gain feedback and listen for areas in which to improve, ways that people of different races could feel included and see themselves at a church led by a white pastor. I participated in some of those candid conversations when African American and Hispanic members talked about their experiences, about the lack of people of color in leadership and on staff. The good thing about it: changes did gradually come. Leaders listened and groomed Black and Hispanic members for leadership positions. Not only did singers standing on stage begin to mirror the congregation's growing diversity, but so did their song choices. Contemporary Christian songs often segued into popular choices from Black gospel charts.

But now, it seemed, this idea that my grandfather's story proved somehow too raw for the masses caught me off guard. I asked for clarity: "Are you saying I shouldn't talk about racism at the church?"

"No, no, I'm not saying that," he said. He just felt I should know the discomfort that he and some other white members felt, he said.

I appreciated him for sharing these feelings, I said to end the call. Then I considered his words for a long time. He and I had talked on several occasions. He'd shared his own diverse experiences with African Americans, as well as some ways that he'd been ostracized in life. He was no closeted racist, so I chewed over this idea of white discomfort. I'd attempted to deliver a message with a universal theme of overcoming loss and failure, but racism still dominated some views of the story. Perhaps racism remains so rife in America, so engrained in the DNA of this country, that it will be more uncomfortable to discuss than productive for some—that is, until we truly do overcome it, until the truth of our past becomes only a reminder that no longer stings.

It's OK to be uncomfortable—at least that's what I concluded. Adults professing to speak truth to the masses should take time to think about racism, allow themselves to be bothered, to squirm at the facts of ancestors' actions. The church leader saw this unsettledness as a problem, but I deemed it a necessity. Discomfort can signal areas where we need to heal, improve, and grow. It is the intersection of truth and apathy, a confrontation with someone else's pain. When it comes to racism, white discomfort may indeed be the sign that they've been comfortable for far too long, especially in the church. Segregation in the pews today is residue from racism that proliferated in churches years ago. White preachers condoned slavery and white superiority and shunned the very Negroes they'd converted to the faith from worshipping alongside them. Black people created their own separate churches and read hope into the scriptures that white supremacists misinterpreted and politicized for the sake of their own privilege. Now, for the sake of healing and restoration, church leaders can't simply avoid talking about the past and behave like racism is over. Their discomfort is a clear sign that it's not over at all.

I made one big mistake in the situation with that church leader, though. After our phone call, I dropped the discussion entirely. I didn't want to be seen as a rabble-rouser. We never talked about it again. I didn't even tell friends, Black or white, worrying that some might view him negatively. In retrospect, I became the woman who avoids telling her truth to protect someone else, for fear of stirring tension or being outcast. I eventually regretted not taking a stronger stance on how the authenticity of Granddaddy's experience could positively affect lives in our modern landscape. Deeper discussion might have stoked growth among leaders, the congregation, and me, too. In honesty, I wasn't ready for the critique. I needed to grow, to come to a place of reckoning with the traumatic residue of Granddaddy's story, to build up my own understanding and confidence in its relevance today.

—⚉—

CHAPTER SIXTEEN

VENGEANCE IS HIS

WILLIE JAMES was the first of the siblings to move to Fort Wayne, heeding the call of a cousin who had made the journey. Two of Granddaddy's daughters stayed in other parts of Alabama. Robert Lee ultimately settled in Buffalo, New York. Langhorn B. moved away for a while, then moved back home and lived his last days at the family homestead. But most siblings followed Willie James, one by one, to the Midwest, traveling along a string of roads that led to Fort Wayne. Howard came after Willie James and soon encouraged my mother to relocate. He made the trek to pick her up and dropped her off at that house on Masterson with her cousins. The other brothers and sisters eventually came, too, staying for a time with my parents before getting jobs and places of their own. In Fort Wayne, we celebrated major holidays together, grilling ribs for the Fourth of July, baking turkey for Thanksgiving and ham for Christmas.

We all made the twelve-hour drive back down south at least once a year. That's because, after Granddaddy and Langhorn B. died, my uncle Israel organized the first family reunion. We should come together for happy times, not just funerals, he said. So we did. Every year brought a two-day event with home-cooked soul food, dancing, card playing, smack talking, storytelling, and much laughter. The reunion soon grew to include a broader extended family network, and we'd travel to different US cities where Page relatives had settled. The journeys became our summer vacation trips—to Florida, New York, Maryland, and Georgia, to different cities in Indiana and Alabama. We met my mother's cousins—from Big Mama's side and Granddaddy's side—and their kids too. We always held the traditional fish fry, meet-and-greet night, and the finale banquet. Sometimes we did group tours or activities, as well, to

Relatives pose for a group photo during a Page family reunion. In the front row, Big
Mama is surrounded by her daughters. *From left*: Ossie Mae, Julia, Margaret "Big
Mama," Emma, Margaret, Cora. *Page family photo*

a state park, to Niagara Falls, to shopping malls, to the Martin Luther King Jr.
National Historic Park. As a child, I loved the travel, gathering with cousins,
seeing out-of-town relatives I'd never met, and hearing the previous generation
tell how we were all connected.

Back in Fort Wayne, other Black families spoke of similar experiences with
their own down-south reunions. Hoosier classmates, meanwhile, relayed much
different scenes of summertime, of their nuclear family travels to American
landmarks, beaches, or other tourist destinations. Some cultural differences
crystalized for me when talking with a white classmate who said she didn't really know her cousins. My face scrunched in confusion, and I couldn't help but
ask more questions. *You don't spend the night at your cousin's house? You don't
have family reunions?* No, she said, just as confused by my bonds of kinship as
I'd been by her lack of them.

Relatives pose for a group photo during the Page and Warren family reunion activities in Fort Wayne in 2017. *Courtesy of Gradlin Pruitt*

But before my own revelations about culture and kinship, even before our first official family reunion, the Pages had traveled again down south to visit the place they still called home. On this particular occasion, Willie James recalled, the brothers were sitting in front of a fire, so it may have been Christmastime. And Granddaddy finally broke his silence. By then, some years passed since they got him, and a lot had changed. For one, the family moved from Browns to Uniontown, a few miles west, where Big Mama's ancestors owned land. Since Granddaddy couldn't use his right arm, he taught his younger sons to build the new house on a plot there, directing them along the way, just as his father had guided him. This is the house lodged in my memories. Here, some of the brothers gathered around Granddaddy in that front room, the one with the straw-back chairs, the beds, and the fireplace. Not long before, a tragic mishap got people talking all over town. Remember the man whose car Granddaddy had rear-ended on the bridge, the one Granddaddy's frat brothers had paid off? That man's son had died in an accident, the details of which aren't clear today.

Several of the Page brothers and cousins moved to Fort Wayne and traveled back to Alabama for family visits. *From left*: Howard Page, David Warren (cousin), Willie James Page, Robert Lee Paige, and younger brother Israel Paige, also known as "Junior." (Some brothers added an *i* to the spelling of their name.) *Page family photo*

One uncle said it involved a fall and a silo; another mentioned a storage bin, while others didn't recall any details. They just knew something had taken the son's life, and people from Browns to Uniontown had this on their minds.

The calamity settled in Granddaddy's mind a bit differently than some others. For him, it signaled a time for revelation. That father, Granddaddy said, had been the one in the car, shoulder to shoulder with those kidnappers in 1959. Even with his head pressed to the floorboard that day, Granddaddy easily judged the twists and turns leading to the man's farm. Now, without anyone taking a single step for revenge, that man had suffered the worst kind of pain anyone could—the tragic death of his own son. No one, not even Dave, saw the need for a common man's justice exchanged with fists and cuss words now. Granddaddy's silence had kept his family intact, but tragedy took that kidnapper's son and likely stole his peace right along with it.

For years, I tried to document this kidnapper's identity, if for nothing more than my own satisfaction. I used nuggets of information from my uncles to search ancestry records, newspaper articles, and any electronic property documents accessible. I found clues and interesting potential connections but nothing absolute. The uncertainty rested partially in that my relatives pronounced the man's name phonetically, but none of them had ever spelled it or seen it in print. Too many variations and possibilities prevented drawing a conclusion. I settled that I didn't need to know, not right now. The whole scandal loomed much larger than that guy. The true kidnappers were the racial injustices of a system that let it happen, that let it go unpunished—that persist in our nation today.

During my third trip to the Dallas County Courthouse, I entered through the same door I had on my initial visit when a court file spelled out the details of Granddaddy's case. A different clerk stood behind the counter this time. She seemed preoccupied with other work for the day. I told her I wanted to look for files we may have missed about the case on my first trip. This time, she directed me to the courthouse basement to scour boxes of files for myself.

The dim, dusty cellar played with my fears of rodents and crawly things. I entered, talking and singing to myself, making noise to scare off potential critters. No matter what, I couldn't turn back, so I settled in, pulled boxes from shelves, and reviewed files one by one. I lost track of time in my search for anything that showed the slightest movement in Granddaddy's case, anything that the first clerk had missed. The most interesting document I found rested in a file named "Consolidated Docket and Fee Book." There, I spotted notes about the case's progress through the court system. Granddaddy took no action after the kidnapping, but the case remained open until 1963 when Lee motioned for its dismissal. The court granted his motion and decided that the plaintiff, Granddaddy, would be "taxed" for court costs. An order executed against Granddaddy in July 1968 mandated that he pay twenty-six dollars for clerk's fees, sheriff's fees, and a trial tax.

Why Dallas County officials waited five years after a judge formally dismissed the case to try and collect the fee is an unanswered question. The delayed effort proved too late, though. By then, the family had moved from Browns and built the house in Uniontown, Perry County. Officials didn't have a new address. The clerk put a final stamp on the docket, "execution returned no property found."

Less than a year later, on January 9, 1969, Brantley Lee died of a heart attack at age fifty-nine. A week after that, the local registrar received and dated his death certificate for archiving. The stamp on his certificate reads January 16, 1969—the tenth anniversary of the civil trial that never was.

SIX DECADES AFTER THEY GOT DADDY, 2021

"I think racism still exists, but it's more of a subconscious thing," my fifteen-year-old nephew David was saying. "A lot of white people, it's more like they think down on us. . . . It's kind of engrained," he said. "It's just in them."

David and my other nephew, AJ, had listened intently as I told them my grandfather's story and other experiences their parents and I had endured growing up. Like our parents, we had failed to share these stories with the next generation. We cautioned them about racism in general terms and pointed to the latest news stories, while tucking our firsthand challenges to the backs of our memories. We wanted them to enjoy the freedoms of America but also to be careful, mindful of their brown-skinned bodies and how some would see their color as a deficit to be overcome. But now, we delved into these issues. We had to. Racial tensions in America and the tenor of hatred in recent years forced us to recall past microaggressions and to be frank with those coming after us.

David never saw any Klansmen in hoods, other than on television. Too young to drive, he hadn't feared for his life during a traffic stop, although his parents prepared him with the traditional tutorial to Black children in case police pulled them over. Keep your hands on the steering wheel and in view at all times. Don't reach for or grab anything—and that means anything—from anywhere.

"If I got pulled over, I would get my license and registration," said, AJ, eighteen. "I'd automatically have that out." Gripping an invisible wheel, he positioned his hands at the classic ten and two positions. "I'd have my hands on the steering wheel and be like, 'Hello, officer, what can I do for you today?'" he said, overenunciating.

David rounded out the verbal guidebook. If the cop showed any sign that he might be anxious or antsy, he said, "Just put your hands out the window and let them arrest you."

Police brutality, "that definitely exists," AJ said. "It is what it is. It's there." But since neither he nor David had licenses at the time, the scenario felt disconnected for them. My nephews could not fully relate to the barbs that pricked us in the 1980s and 1990s either. To them, Facebook was a relic of the past for people like their parents, uncles, and aunts. My story of how a former friend and Bible study partner unfriended me on Facebook after I challenged a racially tinged post and her not-so-subtle references to Black people and "culture" would mean little to them. Their age group, generation Z, used Instagram, Snapchat, TikTok, and other social media platforms.

Great-grandchildren of Israel and Margaret Page play a game of foosball during a family reunion in Fort Wayne in 2017. When playing virtual video games with strangers, they said they had been called "nigger" by anonymous gamers. *Sharon Tubbs photo*

"So have you experienced blatant racism or prejudice?" I asked the question almost rhetorically. I thought the answer would be no since I saw their generation as much more progressive and inclusive than mine. I liked the idea that they might never be followed around a store, threatened and told to leave town, or feel the tension of seeing a white supremacist face-to-face.

"I mean, has anyone ever called you the n-word?" I asked, thinking I already knew the answer.

Then David said, "Oh, all the time." He shrugged.

Maybe he didn't hear me clearly, I thought. I repeated the question.

Yes, he said, assuring me. He'd been called a nigger on numerous occasions by his own peers. This, he said, is how he knew racism persists, but in a different way than our old-school stories.

"Where?" I asked.

"On the game," he said matter-of-factly. "It happens all the time."

At the time, my nephews often played video games for recreation. Video gaming had evolved since my youth, and players could connect with others online and form teams or competitions. In these virtual parties with strangers who enjoyed the anonymity of the internet, David experienced the same racist name-calling and belittling in the twenty-first century that has existed in America for more than four hundred years.

Interestingly, avatars often represented the players, so they couldn't see each other's faces. David says his voice, a deeper tone than some of his white peers, always gave him away. He recalled making a wrong move once while playing with a team of unknowns. A white guy on David's own team grew frustrated and called him a "stupid nigger." Another time, he browsed a list of "parties" for another popular game and came across one with a curious stipulation for people to join. "No Blacks allowed," the listing said. David joined anyway to see what would happen. "Are you Black?" someone asked, after he spoke. "Yes," David said. "Can't you read? I said no niggers!" The organizer then booted him out of the party.

Not exceptions, these practices are common online when playing with strangers, my nephews said.

"I've experienced it multiple times where I was playing, and I'll say something, and a white person will say, 'Shut up, nigger,'" David said.

AJ chimed in, saying he'd been called the same during gaming parties and chats. He dismissed the intended insults and laughed out loud to anger the person. "Stuff like that is funny when it happens to you over the game," he said. "I'm not about to get mad that somebody across the country called me a nigger," he said. "It's funny because they think we're going to get mad, but we don't get mad. . . . The only objective is to, like, get us in our feelings, get us upset."

Online video games are not the only venue where the behavior breeds. David showed examples of blatantly racist posts on Instagram and videos on TikTok. One post decried the supposed physical grotesqueness of Black women, calling us "sheboons." Another short video featured a Black woman satirizing the arrival of a Black family to a white neighborhood. The video showed the woman at a window, saying "niggers" and dramatically gasping at the sight of a Black couple moving into a house across the street. The Black creator mocked white women's reaction and the use of "nigger" behind closed doors in modern times.

For David, these experiences signaled the depth of racism in our nation. The same people who comfortably called him names under the guise of their gaming pseudonyms and the protection of the internet would likely smile at him in school hallways. They might be "model students," he said, students whose parents toted briefcases and spoke with political correctness.

"So that's what I mean that it's kind of like engrained," David said. "If it's like in real life, they're not going to say it, but if it's a game, they're going to say it."

I paused to absorb their reality. Despite the protest marchers singing "We Shall Overcome," federal legislation to ensure equal rights, and multicultural megachurches with people praising a God who created us all, Black youth in the twenty-first century still face the prospect of being called niggers. In fact, some see it as common, a brush-off-your-shoulder moment to be anticipated whenever their white opponents hide in anonymity. This next generation of my family chose to push the experiences to the backs of their minds, just as my brother and his friends did when they got back on the bus in Martinsville nearly four decades ago. Just as my sister and I did when scurrying out of that clothing store. This ability to keep going is good, I know. It has allowed us—allows the next generation—to focus on goals without bitterness or hatred that consumes. Still, these microaggressions don't go anywhere through our silence. They remain, lying dormant, only to be recalled and processed years from now when we mature.

"So do you feel you have an equal chance of success in life?" I asked. "Equal to your white classmates?"

"Not equal, but we do have a good opportunity," David said. "They have it better. I don't know how to go deep into it, but they definitely have it better. . . . I think it may be easier for white people to advance in rank or position. You don't see a lot of Black people in a lot of [prestigious] positions, things like that."

"They're out there, more than you think," said AJ, a recent high school graduate. AJ did not see his Blackness as a hindrance, despite the anonymous critics on the internet. He had several white friends during his younger school days. He remembered a special group in which he participated where the high school brought in African American professionals to talk with a select group of students as successful role models. "I don't think it's as hard for Black people as we're making it seem nowadays."

At least that was his perspective. Grandaddy might compare our modern lives to his and say the same. And, really, that is the hope of every generation, isn't it? We hope that success is not as hard for our children and their children's children, that the hardships we worked so diligently to overcome were, indeed, overcome. Immigrants hoped for as much when they settled in America from Europe. They wanted to establish a great land for themselves, for their families and descendants. This had to be the hope of Irish immigrants who fled famine in their native land in the mid-nineteenth century, searching for a place that could sustain life, where they could thrive. Jewish people who eventually settled here hoped, too. They wanted freedom, socially and economically, in America.

For young Blacks coming up today, like my nephews, life in America does not compare to the adversity Prince Page or his son Israel Sr. endured. The strides that we've made came from determination and undying faith, a belief in God, and hope that America's Declaration of Independence would someday ring true for all of us: *We hold these truths to be self-evident, that all men are created equal, that they are endowed by their Creator with certain unalienable Rights, that among these are Life, Liberty and the Pursuit of Happiness.* Throughout history, certain heroes and sheroes have held America accountable to those words. They are the names in history books and celebrated during Black History Month. Others, meanwhile, have tried to do the same, but with lesser or no change. Some in America have continued to trample on the words of this founding document. Yet the so-called failures that resulted still count toward the goal of equality, nonetheless. Those stories, like Granddaddy's, spur future generations to take the baton and run on farther toward justice. They resonate with descendants like me.

As much as I claimed this as Granddaddy's story, then our family's story, I see now that it is even more than that. It is also the story of Brantley Lee and those kidnappers. It is the story of the county commissioners and white residents of Browns and Uniontown, the ones who watched these events play out but who did not step in. It's the story of ministers, landowners, and regular townsfolk who should have joined in the fight for justice, as did Cecil Radford, the Dallas County Bar Association, or even civil rights reporters who scurried to include Black voices in their articles. In the racist South that deemed him inferior, that oppressed him, that stifled his ability in many ways to fight back, Granddaddy needed people with privilege, power, and a voice to deem his story worth telling and speaking up for. He needed them to join in the battle for the sake of good and justice. In many ways, our evolution in this country—from the civil rights movement to Black Lives Matter protests; from niggers, coloreds, and Negroes to Blacks and African Americans—is merely a collection of stories that call for respect and equality for all in America.

Granddaddy's story, then, is a piece of that collection. It speaks of his heart and of those who stood on the wrong side of history. For him, the questions were: Would he find more Cecil Radfords who step up for the sake of justice? Or would there be more Mary Cains, people who try to erase the effects of slavery, telling themselves that Negroes had adequate opportunity to fight their own battles and liberate themselves after four hundred years of oppression? Would they tell themselves they had no responsibility to participate in change, because they weren't around back then? Would they be like the modern-day nonprofit leader, fighting for the rights of the underserved by day while quietly clinging to white privilege, begrudging the self-sacrifice necessary for a greater good?

Even worse, would they become erasers who purge these stories from our historical cache, scrubbing away the fulness of our pasts—"our" being those of us whose stories don't fit the paradigm of all that is fair and just in America? These erasers tried to diminish the Native American story to elevate the idea that Christopher Columbus "discovered" America. They deny that millions were tortured and murdered in the Holocaust. They fail to mention the existence of Japanese internment camps in the annals of history. They forget about the federal government's role in the roots of segregated housing and creating inner city ghettos in America. They downplay the lasting effects and generational trauma of the castrations, lynching, and horrific murders of Black men and women in our history. They tire of people discussing such sober topics and ignore the pain around them, hoping it will all just go away.

Yet the erasers have not been successful, not fully. These truths emerge from the grave, rising to be told so that new generations will know from where we've come and how history continues to shape who we are and where we stand. They resurrect, so we might avoid repeating past evils and work together to create a better future. Though some say, "Let it go" or "That was then, this is now," the stories will not stay buried. They can't—they're not really dead yet. Just like Granddaddy's experience, their blood still pumps through modern race relations and oppression and hatred. And so, the stories of our past, mine and yours, peek at us from newspaper pages and court documents. They whisper through the traumas of our elders and ourselves, telling us that the "they" who "got Daddy" were not confined to four men in a car. No, "they" includes the many others who allowed him to get gotten in the first place. "They" are those who sat idly by afterward, benefitting from the privilege that propelled tragedy to take place. Now these same stories, like ours, come alive again, not for unnecessary shame but because they are the leavening agent for healing. The kind of healing that stirs each of us when we process the truth of our history. With true healing, we expose true struggle and overcoming strength; we rest in humility and cherish accountability. And, through our successes—and our failures, too—we are girded by the sustaining power of faith.

NOTES

*Information is based on documents from the Circuit Court of Dallas County
    Alabama:
Israel Page v. Brantley Lee, Case No. 6442, Circuit Court of Dallas County,
    Alabama.
*Consolidated Docket and Fee Book, Civil Division, Circuit Court, Dallas
    County, Alabama, Case No. 6442.
Information from Ancestry.com was used throughout this project.

INTRODUCTION

Pages x–xiii
    Information about cultural trauma:
    Alexander, J. C. "Culture Trauma, Morality and Solidarity: The Social Con-
struction of 'Holocaust' and Other Mass Murders." *Thesis Eleven* 132, no. 1 (2016):
3–16. https://doi.org/10.1177/0725513615625239.
    Clemmons, Jacquelyn. "Black Families Have Inherited Trauma, but We Can
Change That." Healthline.org, Aug. 26, 2020. https://www.healthline.com/health
/parenting/epigenetics-and-the-black-experience#The-path-to-healing.

Pages xi–xii
    Ahmaud Arbery, Breonna Taylor, and George Floyd were African Americans
killed by whites in 2020 whose deaths sparked a political and emotional firestorm
across the country. After the murder of George Floyd by police officer Derek
Chauvin, protests erupted nationwide, with people of all ethnic backgrounds
calling for justice. The *Star Tribune* in Minneapolis won a Pulitzer Prize for
its coverage of the Floyd murder. Other suggested sources include the *Atlanta*

Journal-Constitution for the Arbery case and the *Courier Journal* in Louisville, Kentucky, for more information about Taylor.

Page xii

Information about implicit bias in the medical industry:

Hirsh, Adam T., Nicole A. Hollingshead, Leslie Ashburn-Nardo, and Kurt Kroenke. "The Interaction of Patient Race, Provider Bias, and Clinical Ambiguity on Pain Management Decisions." *Journal of Pain* 16, no. 6 (June 2015): 558–68. https://www.jpain.org/article/S1526-5900(15)00596-9/pdf.

Rapaport, Lisa. "Nonwhite Patients Get Less Pain Relief in U.S. Emergency Rooms." *Physicians Weekly*, July 2, 2019. https://www.physiciansweekly.com /nonwhite-patients-get-less/.

Sabin, Janice A. "How We Fail Black Patients in Pain." Association of American Medical Colleges, Jan. 6, 2020. https://www.aamc.org/news-insights/how-we-fail -black-patients-pain.

Pages xii–xiii

Information about the Tuskegee experiments and eugenics, past and present:

Carmon, Irin. "For Eugenic Sterilization Victims, Belated Justice." MSNBC. com, June 27, 2014. http://www.msnbc.com/all/eugenic-sterilization-victims -belated-justice.

Dorr, Gregory Michael. "Eugenics in Alabama." Encyclopedia of Alabama, Oct. 10, 2007, last updated Apr. 21, 2015. http://www.encyclopediaofalabama.org /article/h-1367.

Nix, Elizabeth. "Tuskegee Experiment: The Infamous Syphilis Study." History. com, May 16, 2017, updated Dec. 15, 2020. https://www.history.com/news /the-infamous-40-year-tuskegee-study.

O'Toole, Molly. "ICE Is Deporting Women at Irwin amid Criminal Investigation into Georgia Doctor." *Los Angeles Times*, November 18, 2020. https://www .latimes.com/politics/story/2020-11-18/ice-deporting-women-at-irwin-amid -criminal-investigation-into-georgia-doctor.

Powel, Aisha. "Mississippi Appendectomy: The Decades Long Practice of Sterilizing Poor Black Women." Theblackdetour.com, Feb. 25, 2019. https://theblack detour.com/mississippi-appendectomy-the-decades-long-practice-of-sterilizing -poor-black-women/.

Treisman, Rachel. "Whistleblower Alleges 'Medical Neglect,' Questionable Hysterectomies of ICE Detainees." National Public Radio, September 16, 2020. https://www.npr.org/2020/09/16/913398383/whistleblower-alleges-medical -neglect-questionable-hysterectomies-of-ice-detaine.

Page xiii

Infant and maternal mortality rates in the United States and Indiana:

Chapman, Sandra. "Indiana Has One of the Worst Rates for Childbirth-Related Death." WTHR.com, June 20, 2019. https://www.wthr.com/article/indiana-has -one-worst-rates-childbirth-related-death.

Gibson, London. "Hoosier Mothers Die in Childbirth at Same Rate as Women in the Gaza Strip." *Indianapolis Star*, Oct. 28, 2019. https://www.indystar.com /story/news/health/2019/10/28/maternal-mortality-indiana-childbirth-death-rate /3899877002/.

Page xiv

Surveys about religion and African Americans:

Diamant, Jeff. "Blacks More Likely Than Others in U.S. to Read the Bible Regularly, See It as God's Word." Pew Research Center, May 7, 2018. https://www.pew research.org/fact-tank/2018/05/07/blacks-more-likely-than-others-in-u-s-to-read -the-bible-regularly-see-it-as-gods-word/.

Masci, David. "5 Facts about the Religious Lives of African Americans." Pew Research Center, Feb. 7, 2018. https://www.pewresearch.org/fact-tank/2018/02/07 /5-facts-about-the-religious-lives-of-african-americans/.

*See note in chapter 2 for reference to the northern migration of African Americans.

CHAPTER 2

Pages 5–6

The Great Migration, also known as the Black Migration, generally began between 1910 and 1916 (depending on which expert you ask) and ended in 1970. During this time, an estimated six million Black people left the nation's southern states to relocate to the North, West, and Midwest. When the exodus began, the majority of Black Americans lived in the South. By 1970, more Black people lived outside of the South for the first time in US history. Fort Wayne, Indiana, was among the midwestern cities where southerners settled during that time. However, they were not the first Black people in the city. Black residents, including entrepreneurs, as well as factory workers and others, were established in the city for years prior to the migration period.

Editors of Encyclopaedia Britannica. "Great Migration: African-American History," Encyclopedia Britannica Online, updated June 30, 2021. https://www .britannica.com/event/Great-Migration.

Platt Boustan, Leah. *Competition in the Promised Land: Black Migrants in Northern Cities and Labor Markets*. Princeton, NJ: Princeton University Press, 2017.

US Census Bureau. "The Great Migration, 1910 to 1970," Census.gov, updated Sept. 13, 2012. https://www.census.gov/library/visualizations.html.

Wilkerson, Isabel. *The Warmth of Other Suns: The Epic Story of America's Great Migration*. New York: Vintage, 2011.

CHAPTER 3

Pages 11–12
The weather on July 15, 1954:
Geiger, Peter, and Sondra Duncan, eds. *Farmers' Almanac 2014*. Almanac Publishing. Accessed December 11, 2013. http://www.farmersalmanac.com/weather-history/.

Page 15
Information about the Gee's Bend development:
Stevens, Kyes. "Gee's Bend." Encyclopedia of Alabama, March 9, 2007. http://www.encyclopediaofalabama.org/article/h-1094.

Pages 21–23
Information about the car crash:
Capell, Arthur. "Negro Prays for Lord's Guidance in Traffic Case." *Selma Times-Journal*, Jan. 18, 1959, A1.
Selma Times-Journal. "Three Injured in Crash at Browns: Crash First of Year at Intersection." July 16, 1954, A1.

CHAPTER 4

Page 27
For information about the International Harvester and other factories in Fort Wayne, see archives in the *Journal Gazette* newspaper.

Pages 27–28
Reasons for migration from the South to the North; 75 percent of Blacks from southern central states moved to the Midwest:
Boustan, Leah Platt. *Competition in the Promised Land: Black Migrants in Northern Cities and Labor Markets*. Princeton, NJ: Princeton University Press, 2017.

Page 32
Information about white flight and discrimination among employers:
Boustan, Leah Platt. *Competition in the Promised Land: Black Migrants in Northern Cities and Labor Markets*. Princeton, NJ: Princeton University Press, 2017.
Rothstein, Richard. *The Color of Law: A Forgotten History of How Our Government Segregated America*. New York, NY: London. Liveright Publishing Corp., 2018.

Page 32
Information about the Historic Old Fort:
City of Fort Wayne, Parks and Recreation. "Historic Old Fort." Accessed Mar. 1, 2022. http://www.fortwayneparks.org/index.php?option=com_content&view=article&id=26&Itemid=43.

Page 34

Good Times was an American sitcom that aired from 1974 to 1979, starring Esther Rolle and John Amos. The low-income Black family overcame challenges from their apartment in the projects, while still finding occasions to laugh and love. *Three's Company*, a sitcom that aired from 1976 to 1984, starred John Ritter and Joyce DeWitt, among others. Roommates, two women and one man, encountered funny situations and hijinks while sharing a California apartment.

Internet Movie Database (IMDb):

Good Times: https://www.imdb.com/title/tt0070991/.

Three's Company: https://www.imdb.com/title/tt0075596/?ref_=fn_al_tt_1.

CHAPTER 5

Page 35

Information about Black hospitals:

Ward, Thomas J. "Black Hospital Movement in Alabama." Encyclopedia of Alabama, Aug. 24, 2009, last updated May 5, 2022. http://encyclopediaofalabama.org/article/h-2410.

Pages 35–36

Information about the car crash:

Capell, Arthur. "Negro Prays for Lord's Guidance in Traffic Case." *Selma Times-Journal*, Jan. 18, 1959.

Selma Times-Journal. "Three Injured in Crash at Browns: Crash First of Year at Intersection." July 16, 1954, A1.

Pages 36–37

In the Bible, God changes Jacob's name to Israel and brings meaning to the name:

Genesis 32:28.

CHAPTER 6

Page 45

The author Isabel Wilkerson mentions "sister cities" between the South and North in the United States, in reference to the Great Migration:

Wilkerson, Isabel. *The Warmth of Other Suns: The Epic Story of America's Great Migration*. New York: Vintage, 2011.

Pages 49–50

A few references for the trauma of slavery and its effects on corporal punishment:

CNN.com. "Researchers: African-Americans most likely to use physical punishment," CNN.com, Nov. 10, 2011. https://www.cnn.com/2011/11/10/us/researchers-african-americans-most-likely-to-use-physical-punishment/index.html.

Cummings, K. Ward. "Slavery Left a Legacy of Corporal Punishment on Black Communities, Commentary." *Baltimore Sun*, Feb. 4, 2021. https://www.baltimoresun.com/opinion/op-ed/bs-ed-op-0205-slavery-corporal-punishment-20210204-rbdsaywj5vgx3a6gansdq6tf6y-story.html.

Patton, Stacey. "Corporal Punishment in Black Communities: Not an Intrinsic Cultural Tradition but Racial Trauma," American Psychological Association, Apr. 2017. https://www.apa.org/pi/families/resources/newsletter/2017/04/racial-trauma.

Williams, Heather Andrea. "How Slavery Affected African American Families." National Humanities Center, Oct. 2021. https://nationalhumanitiescenter.org/tserve/freedom/1609-1865/essays/aafamilies.htm.

Pages 50–51

A few references for the higher prevalence of stress among Black women:

Collier, Andrea K. "How Stress Impacts Black Women and 10 Tips to Take Control." Healthline.com, Sept. 2019. https://www.healthline.com/health/stress-and-black-women.

Neal-Barnett, Angela. "To Be Female, Anxious and Black." Anxiety and Depression Association of America, Apr. 23, 2018. https://adaa.org/learn-from-us/from-the-experts/blog-posts/consumer/be-female-anxious-and-black.

Richards, Erica Martin. "Mental Health among African American Women." HopkinsMedicine.org, Mar. 2021. https://www.hopkinsmedicine.org/health/wellness-and-prevention/mental-health-among-african-american-women.

CHAPTER 7

Pages 53–54

Talladega Daily Home and Our Mountain Home. "Talladega County Deputy; Two Others Injured in Wreck near Selma Sunday." July 19, 1954, A1.

Talladega News. "Deputy Sheriff Hurt in Wreck Thursday." July 22, 1954.

Page 53

A newspaper reporter interviews Sheriff Earl Howell:

Local populations of Dallas, Perry, and Talladega Counties comes from the 1950 census, US Census Bureau.

Pages 54–55

A newspaper reporter interviews Sheriff Earl Howell:

Talladega Daily Home and Our Mountain Daily Home. "Fascinations, Hardships, Go Along with Police Work." Apr. 28, 1953, 6.

Page 55

On prohibition laws in Alabama:

Downs, Matthew. "Prohibition in Alabama." Encyclopedia of Alabama, Sept. 6, 2019. http://www.encyclopediaofalabama.org/article/h-4126.

Pages 55–56

Stories about Talladega crimes and Brantley Lee's various arrests, investigations, and so on:

Talladega Daily Home and Our Mountain Home. "Animals Mutilate Infant Found at Bon Air." Mar. 2, 1950, 1.

Talladega Daily Home and Our Mountain Home. "Beer, Roscoe Machines Are Seized in Raid." Aug. 26, 1950, 1.

Talladega Daily Home and Our Mountain Home. "Gable Jailed on Vagrancy Charge." Jan. 28, 1953, 5.

Talladega Daily Home and Our Mountain Home. "Justifiable Homicide Ruling Is Returned in Hammer Slaying of Negro Man by His Stepson." Mar. 12, 1953, 1.

Talladega Daily Home and Our Mountain Home. "Sylacaugan's Killer Search Is Broadened: Officers Question Suspect in Georgia." July 15, 1954, 1.

Talladega Daily Home and Our Mountain Home. "Victim's Car Is Found near Winterboro." July 14, 1954, 1.

*Ancestry.com and US Census Bureau records indicate that Benjamin Brantley "B. B." Lee and his wife, Ruby, had one daughter, who is also deceased.

Page 56

Stories about Sheriff Howell firing deputy, Sheriff Howell suicide, and murdered maid case:

Talladega Daily Home and Our Mountain Home. "Sheriff Requests that Deputy Quit." Nov. 4, 1953, 5.

Talladega Daily Home and Our Mountain Home. "Veteran Sheriff Earl Howell Gunshot Victim Here Friday." Oct. 23, 1954, 1.

Pages 56–57

Information about the Mount Vernon asylum and Searcy Hospital:

Kazek, Kelly. "The Curious History of Rapidly Decaying Searcy Hospital, Alabama's Most Historic Site." AL.com, last updated, Jan. 13, 2019. https://www.al.com/living/2016/09/the_curious_history_of_rapidly.html.

Kazek, Kelly. "Spooky, Dilapidated Searcy Hospital Complex Was State's First Asylum for Black Patients." AL.com, last updated, Jan. 13, 2019. https://www.al.com/living/2016/09/spooky_dilapidated_searcy_hosp.html.

Specker, Lawrence. "Searcy Hospital: Fight to Preserve an Alabama Landmark Has Only Begun." AL.com, June 20, 2019. https://www.al.com/news/mobile/2019/06/fight-to-preserve-an-alabama-landmark-has-only-begun.html.

Page 57

Information about car accident and passengers:

Selma Times-Journal. "Three Injured in Crash at Browns: Crash First of Year at Intersection." July 16, 1954, A1.

Pages 57–58

Brantley Lee's charge of reckless driving was dismissed, but he paid $50 fine for not stopping at a stop sign:

Selma Times-Journal. "Negro Guilty on Distilling Count." Dec. 7, 1954, 10.

CHAPTER 8

Page 59

The amount of Israel Page's lawsuit is adjusted for annual inflation of 3.56 percent over the period:

DollarTimes. "Inflation Calculator." Accessed July 24, 2022. https://www.dollartimes.com/.

Pages 61–62

Information about Sheldon Fitts Sr. and family:

Greensboro Watchman. "Solicitor Hare Wins Full Term in 4th Circuit." May 4, 1950, 1.

Selma-Times Journal. "Engagements." *Selma Times-Journal,* June 7, 1959, 15.

Selma Times-Journal. "Marion Plans to Hold Horse Show." *Selma Times-Journal,* May 6, 1955, 3.

Selma Times-Journal. "Sheldon Fitts, Candidate for Solicitor, Has Long History in Legal Profession." Feb. 17, 1950, 8.

Selma Times-Journal. "Up and Down the Town." Aug. 20, 1925, 8.

Selma Times-Journal. "News of Interest in Social Circles." June 15, 1933, 3.

Page 64

Information about the new Talladega sheriff and about Brantley Lee no longer being employed by the sheriff's office:

Talladega Daily Home and Our Mountain Home. "John Robinson Is Sworn in as Sheriff Today." Jan. 17, 1955, 1.

Pages 64–65

Information about Talladega commissioners and negotiations, settlement:

Talladega Daily Home and Our Mountain Home. "Claim Settlement Delayed When Commissioners Couldn't Agree." Aug. 9, 1955, 1.

Talladega Daily Home and Our Mountain Home. "New Commission Approves Claim." Feb. 17, 1957, 1.

Talladega Daily Home and Our Mountain Home. "Pay Request Deferred." Aug. 19, 1956, 1.

Talladega Daily Home and Our Mountain Home. "Varied Matters Come before County Fathers at Meeting." Sept. 11, 1956, 1.

CHAPTER 9

Page 66

The Brady Bunch TV series portrayed the marriage of an architect and a home-maker, each married for the second time and bringing in three children each to form a home of two adults, six kids, and a maid. The family worked through the trials of being a blended home with young children, then teens.

IMDb: https://www.imdb.com/title/tt0063878/

Pages 72, 74

Information about Martinsville, Goshen, and sundown towns:

Crothers, Julie. "Goshen City Council Approves Resolution Acknowledging 'Sundown Town' Past." *Goshen News*, Mar. 17, 2015. https://www.goshennews.com/news/goshen-city-council-approves-resolution-acknowledging-sundown-town-past/article_9db44bd6-cd0f-11e4-948d-8774e13ff2b6.html.

Higgins, Will. "'We Need to Acknowledge It': Martinsville Tries to Remake Its Racist Image," *Indianapolis Star*, Nov. 2, 2017. https://www.indystar.com/story/life/2017/11/02/martinsville-remakes-racist-image/775258001/.

Loewen, James W. *Sundown Towns: A Hidden Dimension of American Racism.* New York: Touchstone, 2006.

Information can also be found at the History and Social Justice website: https://sundown.tougaloo.edu.

CHAPTER 10

Pages 76–78

Information about the Jimmy Wilson case:

Associated Press. "NAACP Hits Death Penalty for $1.95 Robbery in Ala." *Daily Press*, Aug. 23, 1958, 13.

Daily Press. "Negro's Fate up to Court, Gov. Folsom." Aug. 23, 1958, 13.

Dallas Morning News. "Man Faces Death in $1.95 Robbery." Aug. 17, 1958, 9.

Dallas Morning News. "Negro Won't Die over $1.95 Theft." Sept. 30, 1958, 7.

Oregonian. "Folsom Gets Mercy Plea." Sept. 27, 1958, 3.

Plain Dealer. "Robber of $1.95 Due to Die on Oct. 24." Sept. 12, 1958, 4.

Ruark, Robert C. "Death for $1.95 Mustn't Occur." Sept. 22, 1958, 24.

Seattle Daily Times. "3,000 in Canada Ask for Mercy for Negro." Sept. 14, 1958, 1.

Seattle Daily Times. "Death for $1.95 Crime Again Upheld." Sept. 11, 1958, 1.

Seattle Daily Times. "People in the News: Folsom Always Seeks Excuse." Sept. 30, 1958, 7.

Springfield Union. "Appeal Denied to Condemned Negro in Ala." Sept. 12, 1958, 2.

Springfield Union. "Death Penalty Commuted for Jimmy Wilson." Sept. 30, 1958, 1.

Springfield Union. "Negro Attorney Is Hired in $1.95 Death Sentence." Sept. 10, 1958, 23.

Times-Picayune. "Robbery Death Verdict Scored." Aug. 23, 1958, 39.

Trenton Evening Times. "Jim Wilson Reprieved." Sept. 29, 1958, 1.

Page 77

Kellum, Jennifer. "Ammunition for the Reds: Alabama during the Cold War." *AUM Historical Review* 3 (2014). https://www.aum.edu/class/wp-content/uploads/sites/3/2019/09/aumhr-3-contents.pdf

Pages 77–78

Backlash in Alabama against the NAACP:

Brown, Steven P. "NAACP v. Alabama." Encyclopedia of Alabama, Dec. 13, 2017.

National Museum of African American History and Culture. "An Indomitable Spirit: Autherine Lucy." *Our American Story* (blog), Oct. 1, 2014. https://nmaahc.si.edu/blog-post/indomitable-spirit-autherine-lucy.

Phi Alpha Delta Law Fraternity International. "Fred Gray Biography." Accessed Mar. 3, 2022. https://www.pad.org/page/fredgraybio.

Page 79

Sheldon Fitts running for political office:

Greensboro Watchman. "Solicitor Hare Wins Full Term in 4th Circuit." May 4, 1950, 1.

Selma Times-Journal. "Sheldon Fitts, Candidate for Circuit Solicitor, Has Long Experience in Legal Profession." Feb. 17, 1950, 8.

Selma Times-Journal. "Vote for Sheldon Fitts for Circuit Solicitor, 4th Judicial District" (political advertisement). Apr. 16, 1950, 3.

Page 79

Note about African Americans directly after emancipation, during Reconstruction:

Foner, E. "Reconstruction." Encyclopedia Britannica Online, June 30, 2021. https://www.britannica.com/event/Reconstruction-United-States-history

Page 79

Klan members were both Democrat and Republican:

Mendelsohn, Jennifer, and Peter A. Shulman. "How Social Media Spread a Historical Lie." *Washington Post*, Mar. 15, 2018. https://www.washingtonpost.com/news/made-by-history/wp/2018/03/15/how-social-media-spread-a-historical-lie/.

Pages 80–81

Information about Mary Cain and Democratic political views:

Arkansas State Press. "'That "Nigger" Was Lucky He Wasn't Lynched,' Says Defense Attorney." Sept. 5, 1958, 13.

NBC Universal. "Mississippi: A Self Portrait: Mary Cain—NBCUniversal Archives.com" (1966). YouTube video, posted June 9, 2014, by NBCUniversal Archives, 00:00:58. https://www.youtube.com/watch?v=qkRjPMovvoY.

Speer, Lisa K. "Mary Dawson Cain." Mississippi Encyclopedia. Accessed Mar. 3, 2022. https://mississippiencyclopedia.org/entries/mary-dawson-cain/.

Union-Banner. "Radio Broadcast You Will Want to Hear." Oct. 30, 1952, 1.

CHAPTER 12

Pages 94–95

Timeline of civil rights movement events:

History.com Editors. "Civil Rights Movement Timeline." History.com, Dec. 4, 2017. https://www.history.com/topics/civil-rights-movement/civil-rights -movement-timeline.

CHAPTER 13

Page 99

The *St. Petersburg Times* changed its name to the *Tampa Bay Times* in 2012.

Pages 99–100

Tyron Lewis was shot and killed on October 24, 1996. See various news articles at tampabay.com for accounts. Here are a few samples:

Adair, B., and S. Landry. "Police Planned to Get Uhurus off the Street." *St. Petersburg Times*, Nov. 14, 1996, 1.

Roche, T. "Grand Jury: Police Officer's Actions Justified." *St. Petersburg Times*, Nov. 14, 1996, 1.

CHAPTER 14

Pages 104–108

Israel Page quotes and kidnapping information:

Capell, Arthur. "Negro Prays for Lord's Guidance in Traffic Case." *Selma Times-Journal*, Jan. 18, 1959.

Pages 107–108

Text from bar association resolution:

Selma Times-Journal. "Attack on Negro Deplored by Bar." Jan. 25, 1959.

CHAPTER 15

Page 115

The Book of James 1:2–4 (NIV): "Consider it pure joy, my brothers and sisters, whenever you face trials of many kinds, because you know that the testing of your faith produces perseverance."

SHARON TUBBS began her professional career as a newspaper reporter and editor. In a career that spanned seventeen years, she worked briefly for the *Philadelphia Inquirer* then for the *Tampa Bay Times*. As a journalist, she covered various beats that included small-town government, local crime, and national religious issues. Today, Sharon Tubbs is a writer, inspirational speaker, and the director of a nonprofit organization that empowers under-resourced residents in Fort Wayne, Indiana, to live healthier lives.